THE UNHEARD VOICE OF THE HOME HEALTH AIDE

THE UNHEARD VOICE OF THE HOME HEALTH AIDE

THE STRUGGLE FOR REPRESENTATION, RECOGNITION, INDUSTRY INTEGRITY, AND SURVIVAL

EVELYN VARGAS, RN

LIFEWISE BOOKS

The Unheard Voice of the Home Health Aide

The Struggle for Representation, Recognition, Industry Integrity, and Survival

By Evelyn Vargas

Published by:
LIFEWISE BOOKS
PO BOX 1072
Pinehurst, TX 77362
LifeWiseBooks.com

To contact the author: Evelyn-Vargas.com

ISBN (Print): 978-1-952247-92-7
ISBN (Ebook): 978-1-952247-93-4

What cruel mistakes are sometimes made by benevolent men and women in matters of business about which they know nothing and think they know a great deal."[1]

CONTENTS

INTRODUCTION

The elderly do not choose to become ill and dependent on caregivers. Many elderly people are denied the right to optimum home care services because of state and federal regulations governing who is and is not eligible to receive them. Today's government cannot continue ignoring the importance of the growing elder population. It will take people of all ages to support and enhance the safe, healthy independence and mental stability of our aging population.

At the 2002 World Summit, the United Nations discussed and identified three areas of concern: the development of the older person, advancement of health and well-being into old age, and what an enabling supportive system would look like for the aging citizen. An article, "Political Declaration and Madrid International Plan of Action on Aging"[2] explains in-depth the concern the writer had for the future of the aging population. The publication speaks to the aging adult and the lead they are to take in the programs available to maintain optimum body, mind, and spirit.

Medicaid and Medicare have denied many elderly citizens much-needed in-home personal assistance. For those elderly meeting their criteria, this assistance will grant them the privilege of remaining in the comfort of their homes as opposed to a nursing home placement.

My Work in Home Care

Ever since I was a young person, my heart has been drawn to elder care. My first experience in home care came as a field nurse, supervising home health aides (HHAs) and visiting the patients. In February 1995, I responded to an advertisement of a HHA agency seeking a registered nurse (RN) to be a supervisor and instructor for HHAs. I learned early in my nursing career to accept the opportunities for a new experience in nursing when offered. I was primarily trained as an emergency department nurse and received all my expertise in this area of nursing. It was then I realized the emergency room was a revolving door for elderly patients.

I truly enjoyed the provision of elder care in the home done by the certified HHAs. This is where I wanted the elderly in need of care to be maintained in the best of the body, mind, and spirit. The priorities for optimal healthcare were shifting. My reason for moving out of a hospital setting to home care was to make a difference in the long-term health of the elderly.

I quickly filtered through a system that was mismanaged by the agency's higher chain of command and highly overlooked by the Health Management Organization's (HMO's) home assessor. I emerged in my new role as an RN field home care supervisor while simultaneously working as an emergency room nurse.

Suddenly, I had a great deal to learn about the Medicaid and Medicare laws and regulations as they related to the care, or lack of care, of the elderly in their homes. These were never taught or given as protocols to RNs. There seemed to be a disparity as to how an individual was or was not approved for assistance. Documentation of the observations noted by the RN assessor was essential and a key factor for the approval or disapproval of the home care services. The best resolution I found to that disparity was to open my own agency and follow the rules and regulations correctly.

In 2008, I opened Serenity Home Health Services and the School for Home Health Aides. I held on to what I thought was correct protocol. It wasn't until I actually opened the business and understood the standards of practice that I got the courage to teach others in this field to not just hold on to a job but do it with the utmost integrity.

However, as an agency owner, I quickly found the home care system to be very corrupt and fraudulent. It made me question what exactly the role of the HHA was. Upon further investigation and a gut check, the corruption and fraudulent activity gave me no choice but to close my successful home care business in 2015.

Obedience is always better than sacrifice. I am to be obedient to the profession of nursing, and I pray the home care agencies will be obedient to their profession. We must all work with integrity and report wrongdoing even when no one else will. I have a duty to share my experience in this profession of caring for the aging adult. This book will shed light on the cycle of fraud inside home care and call us all to give our elderly, as Medicare and Medicaid recipients, the privilege and right to receive home care services.

CHAPTER ONE

ABOUT HOME HEALTH AIDES AND HOME CARE

To become a certified HHA (Home Health Aide), the individual must complete a seventy-six-hour training course. Different parts of the training course consist of:

Defining Home Services

1. The agency's structure and chain of command
2. Policy and procedures—patient confidentiality, adherence to plan of care

3. Reporting of any change of events
4. Documentation of care administered
5. Body mechanics
6. Medical emergencies
7. Disasters

Understanding the Client

1. Culture and family
2. Body systems and common disorders
3. Aging, death, and hospice care
4. Client care
5. Mobility
6. Personal care
7. Vital signs
8. Special procedures

The education may differ for that specific state. Some agencies will only hire a HHA with a certification from the Board of Nursing or the Board of Education.

Providing the HHAs increased understanding of the agency's structure and their role can promote the proper and legal application of the agency's code of ethics and policies. The objective of explaining the structure of the agency would be to help the HHA protect themself while also preventing the employer from obtaining a liability outcome. HHAs are expected to be compassionate and understanding individuals as they promote health to others.

The HHAs must be provided with an organizational chart, which will give them the chain of command and how to report any abnormal findings in members' homes. They must keep in mind who is in the chain of command. The HHA will take their instructions from the RN who adheres to the proper scope of practice.

HHA as a Caregiver

It is the HHA's job description to assist the elderly and disabled with daily tasks of personal care, light housekeeping, and tasks patients cannot safely do themselves. The HHA often first enters the field of home care because of a desire to help the elderly. They must have compassion and a willingness to work in all kinds of settings, including unfavorable ones.

Caregiver skills include bathing, dressing, feeding, meal preparation, light housekeeping, ambulation, and transferring. These skills are supposed to be approved for those who require hands-on assistance. Many members refuse to express this lack of independence for fear of being placed in a nursing home. This is a very important concern and an area of evaluation that may be overlooked. Will there be a next of kin responsible to the member, or is the member prone to falls and/or deterioration? Further investigation will evaluate whether there is a next of kin.

Who's Eligible and Who's Paying?

The federal and state funding has come up with other ways of maintaining an active lifestyle for our growing elderly population outside of home care. The adult day care has become very popular, but again, it's only for the poverty-stricken elderly. The middle-class population is not eligible for the award of these services. Medicare and Medicaid have failed to understand that the growing population of elderly members may be on the poverty line or just above it. They are all in need of a program that their hard-earned tax dollars should support.

Many of the members above the Medicaid income level are not able to attend an adult day care or request an HHA. This same individual may not have any social support. The growing number of adults living beyond the age of eighty years need to be evaluated because of their needs and not their level of income. The activities of daily living (ADL) and the assistive programs need to be available to all aging adults requesting assistance from the government programs.

Types of Eligibility

The private patient is usually a non-Medicaid recipient who will pay for personal or housekeeping services requested by the individual as it applies to the job description of the home health aide (HHA), personal care assistant (PCA), or companion services. This caregiver doesn't necessarily have to be a certified HHA.

In some cases, the patient has Medicare benefits, but that will not cover the expenses of the home care services. This same individual may need the PCA, but because they are sixty-five or older, they will not be eligible due to the status of the income ineligibility. Even with a slightly higher income, they will not be able to afford the home care services, and yet, they do not meet the criteria for Medicaid-approved home health services.

Why has this been overlooked? Why aren't Medicare recipients allowed the same privileges? In my nursing experience, I have encountered many Medicare individuals who need PCA. These individuals were hard-working citizens of the United States, who today are not eligible for the same services given to their next-door neighbor because of a slightly higher income bracket. They are left struggling month-to-month. The Medicaid recipient has a lower income and has the privilege of home care services.

For Medicare individuals, the cost of living, day to day, is a little above the poverty level (unlike the Medicaid recipient, who is below the poverty level). This gray area of being unable to clear maximum income for Medicaid eligibility excludes a Medicare recipient from receiving the state and federally funded programs approved for the Medicaid beneficiary. Some of the programs are home health services, Meals on Wheels, or adult day care services.

I emphasize, the approval for all the long-term care services, primarily home care services when appropriately assigned as needed for the elderly, will ultimately provide the maintenance of the optimum level of health. Personal care services, when provided according to the administrative code appropriate to that state, can prevent premature deterioration of health where assistance with ADL is required. Long-term care in a home setting can prevent admission to a skilled nursing facility.

Private Pay

This scenario can change when there is a private-pay patient who now lives in exclusive areas of that county. The HHAs either work longer hours or work as a live-in HHA. In caring for privately paying home care and housekeeping services, the paying customer will pay for those services from a hired qualified HHA and another hired individual as a housekeeper.

For the HHA, the work environment would differ from the usual Medicaid recipient who is located in low-income housing as compared to the more affluent customer. The private paying customer may require the same care as the Medicaid member; however, it differs in that the private client can decide what they need and what they pay for. If private-pay members pay only for the care needed, why is the HMO approving care that is not required?

Why Home Care?

Nursing home placement is usually the choice when the next of kin are not available, and home care services are not able to meet the level of care needed during the time allotted by the home care agency. These are the narrowed choices given to the elderly population when their independence in daily activities is compromised. There are times when the choice of staying in the comfort of their homes cannot be given to the individual due to their decision-making abilities and level of independence.

Many of the elderly prefer to be alone in the comfort of their homes. Their greatest fear is being isolated in a nursing home with no contact with the outside world. It becomes imminent that the member must make a healthy choice themself or the next of kin, proxy, or the health professional will decide if the member's medical or mental status requires nursing home placement. If the member is oriented and knows things such as their name, where they are, the date, and who is the current president, their right to stay in their home is granted. This, along with the types of mobilities the member is capable of maintaining in their residence, is also reviewed for independence and deterioration.

The primary goal of the HHA is to maintain the member's optimum level of health while increasing their level of independence. Initially, the members are encouraged to bathe with assistance, dress with assistance, meal preparation with assistance, and range of motion with assistance, with the long-term plan to decrease or cancel any need for personal care assistance. The member should be prepared to discharge from the Medicaid personal care assistance program as their progress increases. As you can imagine, many members refuse independence due to personal comfort and codependency. Housekeeping and companion services are only approved when personal care is the primary necessity for the award of service by the Medicaid regulations.

Safe Independence

Members may not have family members or next of kin to manage their personal care. For the member to live outside of a nursing home, there must be some level of safe independence with their ADL. If living by themselves, the member must have stable mental acuity and mobility, be able to make decisions, and be able to transfer independently (without the assistance of another individual) in and out of a chair or bed.

In other scenarios, the member may be living with a family member who can help with their decision-making ability and the necessary activities related to mobility. The HHA may be approved for the ADLs of the member in the absence of the primary caregiver. But at any time, is this member left alone? Think of them as a child who has certain levels of independence but cannot be left unattended. In many cases, the family must take on the care of the elderly while continuing to support their immediate family.

What Determines Who Needs Assistance?

The three major indicators are: (1) a doctor's order, (2) the completion of the PCA tool by the RN assessor, and (3) a request by a member. In 2011, Medicaid assigned the HMO selected by the member. For example, in the state of New Jersey, there are

HMOs such as United Healthcare, Horizon Blue Cross Blue Shield, Amerigroup, WellCare, and Aetna.

The New Jersey Administrative Code includes all the regulations adopted and published through the New Jersey register, which is Title 10. Human Services, Chapter 60. Home Care Services, Subchapter 3. Personal Care Assistant (PCA) Services, Section 10:60-3.1. The PCA services usually are provided by a certified licensed home health agency or by a voluntary, nonprofit, accredited homemaker agency. The PCA services include personal care, household duties, and health-related tasks performed by a qualified individual in the residence under the supervision of an RN. A physician will write a written plan of care for that individual.

These services are available because the individual now requires long-term care for a chronic condition requiring PCA services, usually reimbursable when provided to Medicaid members in their place of residence. This may include a private home, a rooming house, or a boarding home.

The PCA services described as ADL and performed by the HHA include but are not limited to:

- care of their teeth and mouth, shampooing their hair, shaving, dressing
- bathing in the bathtub, shower, or bed
- use of a toilet or bedpan
- changing the bed linen
- preparing meals

The member's master care plan will indicate which of the above-mentioned categories will be needed per their individual RN assessment. The HHA's responsibility is to document the daily activity administered to the member.

Household duties are those that allow the member to maintain an optimum level of health. Those duties can include light housekeeping (vacuuming, sweeping, dusting), kitchen cleanliness (cleaning the refrigerator, stove, sink, and dishwashing), care of the bathroom (cleaning the toilet, tub, shower, and floor), and personal laundry.

The elderly need a safe exercise program, meal preparation or provision, medication direction, and a supplemental education program that will help them maintain optimum levels of health now—before they are totally dependent on others. Medicaid and Medicare protocols must continually evaluate the program to ensure it can maintain the member's physical stability efficiently. The agency, along with the Medicaid protocols, must adhere to the standard of practice maintained by the accreditation organization.

The member must be encouraged to maintain maximum independence in all levels of care, especially if the member lives alone. There are many cases where we're doing more harm than good because the individual's level of dependency on the caregiver has been promoted instead of encouraging long-term goals of independence through other means. Once the member grows accustomed to having someone care for them, there may be no turning back, as this lifestyle of having free home care and free housekeeping becomes very comfortable.

It is my goal to help you understand the reasons why a person should be awarded such assistance, as well as why they shouldn't be awarded hours for tasks that can be met independently by the individual. Let's look at an example of an HMO case where hours were awarded prior to assessment.

Mr. Thomas

Mr. Thomas is assigned to the home health agency where I am employed. He has a gait disability associated with weakness of the lower extremities and requires a cane. He lives by himself and is requesting a PCA. Mr. Thomas's demonstration shows independent ability of all extremities.

Note: I did not give his age because it will not be the age but the physical disability of the individual that will provide the most accurate outcome for approved or unapproved home care services.

Upon entering the home, I can see he lives in a small one-bedroom apartment. I have not been able to assess any physical limitations. Fifteen hours per week have been approved by the HMO at three hours per day, Monday-Friday from 12:00 to 3:00 p.m. He decided he did not want to get up too early in the morning, so he requested the HHA come at noon. Immediately, an experienced and well-trained RN supervisor would note the following:

1. Good mobility to all extremities
2. Lives alone
3. Oriented to all of his surroundings
4. Does not want morning hours
5. Hours are scheduled Monday-Friday and not on Saturday and Sunday

At this time, the member has bathed independently. When asked how he accomplished bathing without any potential injury, his response was that he had a bar to hold on to and a chair to sit on. In this case, getting in and out of the bathtub did not require assistance.

As the RN supervisor for the member, it is my job to construct a master care plan that accurately instructs the HHA. The short and long-term goals of the member must be made clear. Here are the ones listed for this example:

1. Maintain adequate independence
2. Maintain adequate nutrition
3. Reduce healthcare deficits and limitations
4. Maintain a safe environment

The plan is to successfully execute the goals as quickly as possible in order to discharge the member from the program. However, discharges are rare because the goal might be met but not reported. One of the problems in this example is the assessment should have been completed by the HMO's RN assessor. The assessment tool used by the HMO's RN assessor is based on questions and not the examination of body systems and function.

Another area to evaluate is whether or not this person can cook for themselves. Meal prep is another area that can fall under the assignment of home care. However, having meal preparation only in the morning may leave a member without any meals for the afternoons and evenings. We are then to assume the member will not need other meals.

Mr. Thomas admitted to preparing his own breakfast and lunch, which he can also obtain through the Meals on Wheels program. Once again, what indicators do we have here for Mr. Thomas that would require the award of Medicaid home health care services? He can take care of his breakfast and the preparation of lunch, so apparently, this is not an activity needing support.

Mr. Thomas doesn't think he needs any assistance with meal preparation. He would be given the choice of delivered meals by Meals on Wheels, and many times, he even prepares a meal himself. If Mr. Thomas only has services for Monday-Friday, how are meals prepared or any care rendered on Saturdays and Sundays? If another caregiver involved to assist him was not documented prior to any schedule provided by the home health agency, then it is assumed Mr. Thomas has maximum independence and would only require light housekeeping services.

With the right interventions and tools, the program can be used to avoid injury or early deterioration due to a member's inability to meet the light housekeeping needs. At most, these services, if warranted, should only be one to four hours of service per week, not daily. At maximum, laundry for one individual is done once a week, and for most individuals, once every two weeks. The light housekeeping may consist of mopping, sweeping, vacuuming, and dusting.

The problem here is the strict Medicaid policy stating that assigned hours cannot be used for housekeeping services ONLY. They must be accompanied by personal care. It must be assumed that the assessment was skewed. The member's actual personal care needs did not align with the reasons listed for approved home care services. As a result, the services mentioned by themselves were not approved unless accompanied by a personal need.

In many cases, these are *wants* instead of *needs*. We are all creatures of opportunity, and many try to capitalize on care instead of doing the correct thing. These members want free services, and why not? Everyone else is getting them.

The same can be said of the Medicaid recipient who really doesn't need services for personal care but wants to see if they can get assistance with the light housekeeping. I have come across individuals who admit to this manipulation at the start of the services. Many HHAs are aware but will continue to service them anyway.

This is an area of great concern, and only a few people can really obtain the best reports. The report should be from a non-biased RN through a hands-on physical assessment. This calls for observing the member's general mobility, mental ability, and noting what amount of personal care service is needed. That is the multimillion-dollar question.

The Assigned Registered Nurse and the HHA

The RN with the physician's certification of need will perform an assessment and prepare a written plan of care for the PCA to use in the member's home. In order for a member to be eligible for services, the member must need moderate or greater hands-on assistance in at least one activity of daily living or minimal assistance or greater in three ADL (one of which must require hands-on assistance). The latter part of this regulation will allow the personal care services to provide reminders such as cueing and guiding medical follow-up appointments.

The awareness of the patient's needs is as important as the physician's orders and plan of care. The doctor may order a member to receive services, but does the member meet the requirements according to the New Jersey Administrative Code (N.J.A.C.) 10:60-3.1?[3]

Upon the sixty-day visit to the member's home, or more often as needed, the RN is to initiate that plan of care within forty-eight hours of the start of service and then every sixty days. The purpose of the supervision is to evaluate the assistant's performance for the member indicated on the master care plan. The RN is doing face-to-face supervision to determine whether there is hands-on personal care.

The RN gets little to no orientation as to what is behind the approval of the contract. However, nurses are informed of their job description and the documentation that applies to state protocols required to continue the HMO-approved services.

RNs play a major role in the industry of home care nursing. They are essential, and any concerns expressed to their leaders or field supervisors will hopefully be heard and implemented. The RN can only be productive in the management of their cases when the HHA has been well educated on reporting to their supervisor or home healthcare agency.

How many occurrences in patients' homes may go unreported due to lack of knowledge or because of the fear of the outcome? The HHA may feel a great sense of responsibility to what the assigned patient might have encountered, as in a case of negligence, abuse, injury, or an unusual circumstance in the home. The HHA must gain the confidence and trust of the employer to be able to report an occurrence without any compromise of their self-worth.

Reporting to Adult Protective Services is a required duty of anyone who witnesses abuse, negligence, or any circumstances dangerous to an individual. This is especially important to the HHA who has accepted the responsibility to care for that individual. They must be encouraged to report these incidences as quickly as possible to prevent liabilities against themselves and others. Many have been intimidated by the patient or by relatives. The HHAs are frequently in-serviced on the probable causes reportable to Adult Protective Services.

The HHA, with proper guidance and support, will inform their supervisor of any current or imminent danger to their patient. The HHA must feel confident they will also be guarded against harm for their actions. The agency does have another responsibility, and that is to reassure the member (as well as the HHA) of who is responsible for providing protection to them against any harm.

CHAPTER TWO

THE HOME CARE INDUSTRY

In the past decades, we've seen that Americans are living well beyond the age of eighty and this group is one of the fastest growing populations. In 2002, one study focused on three priority areas: (1) older persons and development, (2) advancing health and well-being into old age, and (3) ensuring enabling and supportive environments. The home care industry is supposed to focus on helping its members be as independent as safely possible, but instead, it encourages the older person to become further and further dependent on the caregiver.

The Medicaid-acquired home health services can be requested with a written doctor's order of the primary care physician (PCP), whereby the physician is to note the areas of deficiencies requiring daily personal care. However, the patient may also request from the PCP a prescription or other written format to be delivered to a desired Medicaid-approved home health agency.

Accrediting Bodies—Who are They?

There are three accreditation bodies: Joint Commission, Community Health Accreditation Program, and the Commissioner on Accreditation for Home Care. An organization providing any form of Medicare or Medicaid services, such as in a home health agency, must meet the qualifications of the federal conditions to participate in home care or a hospice organization. The organization strives to obtain the certification to show the public that they use the best practices.

The accreditation body and its standards must be recognized and approved by the industry's experts. Deregulations create a benchmark by which a health organization will apply to the highest standards of practice for the best possible outcome. One of the three organizations already mentioned has been deemed the authority, which is granted by the Centers for Medicare and Medicaid Services, helping the organization adhere to the home healthcare standards of practice, thereby, maintaining their accreditation status.

Home healthcare business revenues are collected from Medicare, Medicaid, private health insurance, or private pay for service.

Through a coding system, Medicaid will pay for the approved weekly contracted hours. The approval of the contract is initiated with the HMO's approval of a set number of hours for that individual. This becomes the eligibility status that will remain until a review is done by the RN assigned from that member's HMO.

The Personal Preference Program is another form of caregiver approved by the state (Medicaid funded). This program allows the caregiver to be a family member or the like who will then be paid by the HMO under the Medicaid statutes. All the services mentioned under the Medicaid assigned award of hours are fee-for-service.

This is a fee-for-service position, and an RN employed by the member's HMO will complete the assessment. The assessment tool requests a verbal only response from Medicaid recipients on the following categories:

- supportive services
- cognitive status
- ambulation mobility
- ability to transfer
- ability to toilet themself
- ability to perform grooming and dressing tasks
- ability to prepare meals
- ability to perform housekeeping and shopping tasks
- ability to perform laundry tasks

(Note: A physical assessment identifying the motor and mental ability of the member is not part of the tool.) Hopefully, the physical or mental disability has been identified by the medical doctor enforcing the need for the home care services requested. With certainty, I can attest the diagnosis, on many occasions, does not reflect the cause or need for services.

Patient Care Assessment Tool

The Patient Care Assessment tool is of great concern and the primary reason this book was written. There is an array of reasons why the criteria is not being met or why the outcome may be different from one individual to another. The RN assigned by the member's HMO is not required to do a physical hands-on assessment. The Patient Care Assessment tool questions are presented to the member, and their responses are evaluated by the RN. This current tool has major deficiencies, which are largely to blame for many of the inaccurate scores approving the award of services.

Following the initial PCA nursing assessment, the reassessment visit shall be provided at least every six months, when a change of status is reported by the member's physician, or notable discrepancies or changes in health status are reported by the agency. For example, even if the patient has had a change in ambulation, it may not mean they require HHA assistance

The member's insurance plan works for the client and is supposed to ethically, without bias, evaluate the member's home care needs. The nurse may appeal to the patient's request for the sake of maintaining a business relationship. The outcome of the HMO RN assessment can keep a member, as opposed to losing the member to another health insurance that will find a reason to approve the service and gain the member's business.

A member may be approved for two hours per day and up to a maximum of forty hours per week. The assessment areas that can certainly skew the results are meal preparation, bathing, toileting, and transferring. The HHA may have a member who requires two hours per day, usually scheduled anytime between 6:00 a.m. and 8:00 p.m. If the schedule is requested during the morning hours, for example from 8:00 a.m. to 10:00 a.m., the member on many occasions is falsely informed as to the approval of the home care services strictly for housekeeping, but they will many times request the service fraudulently for personal care needs, only to obtain approval of the services used for housekeeping. However, there is a smaller percentage who will use the services as approved by the Medicaid regulations.

The member may be requesting services for assistance with bathing or other personal care activities. Many of the members are aware the services are approved primarily for personal care needs. The members are informed as to what the Medicaid or health insurance RN representative will be assessing and scoring, and they will answer the need to the benefit of getting the services approved.

Therefore, the current assessment tool is basically a guide for the RN assessor, where nursing skills have no input. The tool does not have any basis to prove the member requires the services.

The tool does not allow for any level of performance by which the limitations can be scored. The state needs to implement a preapproval tool where the motor skills and functions are detailed. Additionally, the timeframe of immediate personal care needs due to limitations throughout the twenty-four hours of a day should be specific and not identified as just in the morning or evening.

What I Saw

Early in my career, I had a high regard and respect for the accrediting bodies and the importance they gave to all of the divisions that made up the whole of the agency. I had experienced very knowledgeable surveyors who were able to navigate through office files, HHA health files, personal files, patient files, and the maintenance of policies for the standards of practice necessary to comply with Medicaid protocols. When an agency has less than a hundred patients, their surveyor is able to see if there is continuity in the protocols or if an inconsistency is related to fraudulent activity.

Aside from the protocols, there also is special attention to the sequence of events that requires the gathering of data, which includes the HHA's assignment to the patient's monitoring visits completed by the nurses. The elements require a strategic formula to help the surveyor complete an accurate assessment. This formula is yet to be known. When such a formula is utilized, the surveyor would be able to examine the difficulties the nurse has when trying to organize twenty-five to thirty patients per week in several counties. The nurse does not have a crystal ball to complete an assessment of the member's status prior to being in their home, which would minimize the length of time there.

They are working in the format of an assembly line where the number of members seen is valued higher than any circumstances that may interfere with the scheduled visits. This pressure and stress is placed on the field nurse. I also questioned the Commissioner of Accreditation for Home Care about how the surveyors would not identify certain things such as the patient visit to nurse ratio. Other medical facilities would have to demonstrate there was a standard for the classification or level of care their patient required, as well as how many patients were assigned. Unionized organizations or nursing organizations are not recognized in many states and are the cause for the agency to have little to no professional support.

The agency could have a high patient-to-nurse ratio and comply with accuracy and documentation of the visits in question. In recent years, the same agency fell out of compliance due to a high patient-to-nurse ratio, but this time, the nurse could not complete the visits with the assigned patients. This was identified because the nurses were not actually seeing the members but instead receiving signatures of the members and HHA to comply with the visit.

The nurse adhering to the responsibilities of the agency will do whatever it takes to meet the quota for the day, regardless of the human circumstance that would normally need care and adjustment to the daily schedule of events. The community home care nurse is confronted with many suddenly changing conditions. The nurse is highly responsible to execute a plan for any finding that may accelerate or decelerate the member's health and well-being.

Agencies

Home healthcare agencies come in a variety of sizes and quality. The Medicaid standards of practice and the accreditation must also consider all the objectives or elements required of an agency's organization in addition to the cost of the employer, especially to the RN employee, which is a high expense to the agency. These costs include monitoring visits, time management, performance evaluations, and the home care compliance of the HHA required for continued accreditation. The agency cannot be in compliance without the employed RN.

My experience has shown me the relationship is much different with the smaller more family-type agencies. Smaller agencies often have recognition awards, incentives for growth and development, and bonuses. Nurses and HHAs look forward to the reward system, which enhances loyalty to the company and to their members.

In many larger agencies, respect and recognition are lacking, especially after the mergers, often resulting from the smaller agencies being unable to compete with the larger, multisite agencies.

Today's agencies do not have the strategies or reports required to review nurses, HHAs, and patient schedules. The agency must be able to identify the nurse's field schedule and the other elements that can alter the timely patient visits. The stress to meet a weekly quota opens the potential cause for a topic we will soon discuss—fraudulent activity.

CHAPTER THREE

ASSESSMENTS AND DISCREPANCIES

With the growing elder population comes the need for services provided by HHAs. There are standards and assessments used to help guide the correct number of hours needed to support the member's quality of home life. For example, the HMO has the Patient Care Assessment tool. I have had the privilege of using this tool when working for an assigned HMO approved by Medicaid in the state of New Jersey.

The employed RN for the assigned Medicaid health insurance plans will be asked to do an assessment for a member for the following three reasons:

1. The member requested the services from their medical doctor (MD).
2. A change in health status, where the member is unable to assist themself with the day-to-day personal care activities.
3. The RN agency case manager or the RN HMO case manager assigned to the member has noted a change or evidence of functional impairment that requires an initial home assessment or reassessment.

In general, the assessment is done by the HMO-assigned RN assessor who will complete a no-hands-on assessment by referring to the Patient Care Assessment tool. The RN assessor will gather the information on statements using the tool as a guide. This information will then be evaluated for its contents by an assigned MD. Currently, the PCA tool does not require a physical assessment which can determine factual limitations.

In the summary concluding the assessment, if approved, the member will need the continual assistance of hands-on personal care as required by the New Jersey health code. A final review status of the eligibility by the Division of Disability Services is what will determine the award of the contract, or the number of service hours approved.

The member will score according to a formula of minutes per day multiplied by the number of days requested per week.

> Example: Ambulation—30 minutes maximum per day × 5 days, M–F

This should cause questioning from those awarding the hours per day. If the individual requires assistance with transfers from a bed to wheelchair and will have some level of dependency on the caregiver or is totally dependent on others to be mobile, this member should not be living by themselves or where other supportive care is always available. It is evident that a wheelchair-bound individual will require more assistance with personal care than the approved thirty minutes per day.

Discrepancies

The following are sample scenarios of cases where approved hours didn't match the member's actual needs. This is demonstrated not only by scoring, but also through critical thinking.

Case #1

Female, age seventy-two
Approved fifteen hours per week, M–F
History—Hypertension, diabetes, and hypothyroidism.

- attends a government paid adult day care center
- lives alone
- ambulates independently
- transfers independently
- bathing is done during the morning prior to attending the adult day care and admits she does not need assistance

- has normal bladder and bowel control
- able to cook a light meal for dinner but can use a little help with the preparation
- admits to some difficulty bending to put on garments of the lower extremities
- has normal memory recall and does not need reminding of her medication schedules
- does need reminding of her medical follow-up appointments

In summary, the member does not require an award of hours for the maintenance of optimum health. In my assessment, she would have scored zero in all categories required to meet the state approval.

- Cognitive level: zero minutes
- Ambulation: zero minutes
- Transferring: zero minutes
- Bathing: zero minutes
- Toileting: zero minutes

Cooking assistance request is awarded as per protocol, fifteen minutes per day = one hour and fifteen minutes.

Case #2

Female, age seventy-six
Approved twenty hours per week, M–F

History—Osteoporosis, diabetes type I, hypertension, oriented X3 spheres, and ambulates with cane.

- Cognitive level: zero minutes—member was oriented with her name, place, and time.
- Ambulation: zero minutes—ambulates with some assistance of cane.
- Transferring: zero minutes—able to transfer independently.
- Bathing: zero minutes—able to bath independently, unsupervised by the HHA.
- Meal preparation: scored one hour and forty minutes for one meal (breakfast) per day M–F, as requested by the member. Other meals during the latter part of the day are prepared by the member.

Member states the services are being requested of the HHA for housekeeping purposes only due to the pain of the lower extremities.

The twenty hours were assessed by the HMO RN assessor and approved by the HMO-assigned physician. The awarded hours for the preceding scenario are approved, and the contract is forwarded to the requesting agency.

The RN representing the home care agency's assessment concluded the following summary:

- The member has a steady, non-assisted gait indoors.
- The member will use the cane outdoors for support.

- The member has good mobility to all extremities.
- The member is independent in all levels of personal care.

Meal preparation is the only area of the PCA tool that requires HHA assistance. The issue is that the HHA will not accept assignments for members requiring only one and half hours. If the member is unable to cook for themselves, then who will provide meal preparation for the other meals required for a stable nutritional intake?

The Medicaid PCA program may assist with meal preparation for one of the three meals. They will not and should not award the assigned hours for meal preparation ONLY. The program's need for approval requires a meal-preparation-guided program, which is currently called Meals on Wheels or any other state-approved delivery of frozen meals to maintain optimum nutritional intake when cooking can endanger an individual. The ADLs needed should be assessed and the services provided to maintain the member in their home safely.

Case #3

Female, age eighty-three
Approved twenty-five hours per week, M–F
Member lives with an employed daughter who will attend to her on the weekends.
History—Dementia, hypertension, osteoporosis, hip surgery, diaper dependent, and assisted gait with walker at all times.

This member is likely to score as follows:

- Cognitive level: sixty minutes per week
- Ambulation: fifteen minutes per day M–F
- Transferring: fifteen minutes per day M–F
- Bathing: twenty minutes per day M–F
- Meal preparation: fifteen minutes per day M–F
- Dressing: fifteen minutes per day M–F
- Toileting: fifteen minutes per day M–F
- Light housekeeping: sixty minutes per week (allowed 120 minutes per week divided by the number of persons in the household)
- Grocery shopping: zero minutes (done by daughter)
- Laundry: zero minutes (done by daughter)

My total score for her assessment is ten hours per week.

A Call to Stand Firm

These case discrepancies are only a drop in a bucket of the many awards of services fraudulently approved. The matter is of high concern to many in the healthcare industry. RNs and HHAs must come forward because of their awareness. When are the government officials and policymakers going to stand firm with the complaints others and I have submitted? I have called the accreditation officials known to survey several New Jersey Medicaid-approved home health agencies and their probable ethical and legal intervention.

It is my goal to have the governing body adhere to the New Jersey Administrative Code 10:60-3.1 in the areas of the home health organization awarded hours of service.

- Identify with accuracy the awarded hours per day, time of day, and the weekly total to coincide with primarily the personal care needs.
- The assigned Medicaid-approved home health agency adherence to being ethically correct in the observations, documentation, and reporting of the assessment.
- The member home audit, usually done every six months, should be completed by a Medicaid-employed RN. (Hypothetically speaking, it can be the most effective for a probable nonbiased report.)
- Currently, the home audit is done by the home health provider's RN case manager. Many times, the results are skewed in favor of the member and business interest of the member's health management provider (United Healthcare, Amerigroup, WellCare, Horizon New Jersey).
- Enforcement of the no gifts and bonuses policy, as it may apply to marketing for members. This method has negatively encouraged the HHA employee to convince the member to transfer from one agency to another.
- Revision of the PCA tool to address covert areas of the assessment.

Many years ago, the member's MD would have to have reasons and medical findings as to why the member required home care services. Today, MDs will simply write a prescription with a few diagnoses, which are submitted to the healthcare provider. The methods of approval that commence with the doctor's order lead the healthcare provider down the slippery slope of fraudulent activity, believed by many to be the approved standard of practice as per code N.J.A.C. 10:60-3.1

PCA Nursing Assessment Tool

The PCA tool categories below are used to assess the need for home care services with Medicaid recipients because this is a service only for the Medicaid recipients. Old age comes in all incomes and statuses, and the assessment tool needs to be available to every citizen who meets the mental, physical, and motor disability requirements.

This should be done as frequently as needed or at least every six months by the HMO's RN assessor and as a reporting guide by the home healthcare agency's RN assessor.

Date of assessment: ______________________________

Date of last assessment with current HMO: ____________
____

Date of last assessment with any other HMO: ___________
____

Number of hours: ______________________________

Number of hours with current HMO: _________________

____

Days of week receiving services: e.g.
M Tu W Th Fri Sat Sun

Times of the day receiving HHA services (Can be verified with the master care plan required in the member's home) ______

____

Any denial of services recorded by Medicaid?
Yes ____ No ____

If yes, answer the next question.

Why were services denied? ________________________

____

The member may have been denied services for a variety of reasons, such as:

- improvement in health status and the ability to meet their daily needs safely
- the member's PCP had declared the member does not require home care services
- does not meet the criteria for home care services

- non-Medicaid recipient
- unsafe working environment
- refusal to comply with the agency's protocol and master care plan

The RN assessor is provided the training required to approve or disapprove, providing the tools are used according to the Medicaid standard of practice. Merely using the Patient Care Assessment tool does not accurately assess for the independent and dependent needs of the member.

The tool does not assess the internal home environment. For example, one member may get approved or awarded fifteen hours living in a studio apartment, and another member will be approved the same fifteen hours living in a one-bedroom apartment. Others are living in rented rooms within the home. In this case, there may be a shared bathroom and kitchen where not as much time is needed to care for those common areas because the other individuals are using the same common areas. In essence, the quality indicators for HHA services need to be revised.

Activities of Daily Living

Ambulation

Most members live by themselves or with caregivers not usually present. The maximum of thirty minutes per day is allowed to assist with the pushing of a wheelchair or mobilizing the member from room to room. On assessment, the RN should identify the need for assistance when the HHA is not present.

Does the member require hands-on (contact guard) assistance to mobilize from room to room?

Is the member capable of assisting themself?
_____Yes _____ No (If no, answer the following statement)

Who cares for or assists the member with mobility when the HHA is not available?

Note: A score given for assisted mobility needs to be considered. It is always required when the member is ambulatory and not just thirty minutes per twenty-four hours.

A member who requires assistance with ambulation must have primary caregiver assistance to ensure safety with mobility when the HHA is not present. The current tool does not declare the preceding information to accurately score the member, especially if the member lives by themselves. It needs to be logically assumed that the member should have safe ambulation or live with a caregiver who will continue with ambulation assistance when the HHA is not present.

I have witnessed many cases approved by an HMO, inaccurately assigning an award of service of HHA assistance generally calculated into the total number of assigned hours without factual application. The state- approved PCA tool, used to assess the need for hands-on assistance, fails to accurately measure the response to questions asked at the member's home as it applies to independence vs. dependency on the caregivers. Measuring physical and mental disability must be measured using a tool to obtain mental and physical outcomes by a qualified professional.

The PCP and any other assigned specialty or therapist should be able to identify deficits in the member's motor, physical, and mental assessment. The RN assigned by the HMO does not have the means or directive needed to accurately assess an individual in the privacy of their home. A mental, physical, and motor function evaluation is to be done in a clinical setting or by the healthcare practitioner requesting the home care services.

An example would be a diagnosis of Alzheimer's or dementia. The specialist will conduct a series of tests and analyze and assess memory impairment. Other thinking skills, functional abilities, and behavioral changes should also be required by the qualified professional. The qualified professionals also perform a series of tests to rule out other possible causes of the impairment or outcomes.

The same is to be calculated when the score indicates assistance with a transfer from one location to the next. The tool does not require them to have specific guidelines or motor skills examinations.

In truth, how long does a member need to assist with a transfer into and out of a bathtub? Many elderly live in senior housing, and they do not have bathtubs, only shower stalls. The RN assessor must be required to test the individual ability with all levels of personal care. A change in the current PCA tool should assess if the member requires being mobilized from a chair, bed, wheelchair, or bathtub.

The three areas to score with transfers on the current PCA tool are:

- supervision/limited assistance—up to fifteen minutes/day
- extensive/max assist—up to thirty minutes/day
- mechanical lift/non-weight-bearing—up to forty-five minutes/day

If a member truly requires supervision fifteen minutes per day, then the review must explain why, for the remaining twenty-three hours and forty-five minutes in a day, the member either does not require assistance or has other support assistance in the home. In many home assessments, I have encountered cases where the RN is unable to score the member's capability to complete the transferring skill independently and safely. The tool does not allow the RN assessor to test the recipient for the skill of transferring.

It is all based on a questionnaire. The transferring into and out of a bathtub does not take fifteen minutes. The other types of transferring, extensive and mechanical lifting, mandatorily requires family or other caregiver assistance, supporting the need for thirty to forty-five minutes for extensive transfers, and where the members are required to have caregiver support for the remaining of the twenty-four-hour period.

Meal Preparation

For most recipients, these services are for the preparation of one of the three main meals. The other discrepancy would be the HMO approving a meal preparation Monday-Friday, but it fails to document who is preparing the remainder of the meals, including Saturday and Sunday. However, the questionnaire does not identify who is preparing the other meals.

Accurate documentation will manage the oversight and abuse of home care service. Many of the HHAs will admit that in most circumstances, the member is preparing the other two meals or has the support system who can be responsible for the meal preparation.

CHAPTER FOUR

THE UNHEARD VOICE AND CONCERNS OF THE HOME HEALTH AIDES

HHAs are young and old and mostly of cultures that live within the cities where their members are located. This is largely due to the HHA having minimal training in any other profession. Many HHAs are from other countries where employment in the US is imperative for their own well-being. It has been my experience that many are of a non-white cultural background. This is certainly not to offend or support any one culture, but we must not fail to recognize many of the HHAs are either African American or Latino.

Unstable Work

The HHA may be confronted with challenges and decisions no one should have to endure just for the sake of maintaining an income. They are often the sick taking care of the sick. An HHA's unstable health status is related more to an environmentally stress-induced illness. That, of course, is an illness no one sees until it is evident with some named diagnosis.

It has been my experience to see many of these individuals who are taking care of the elderly unable to maintain maximum health stability due to lack of health coverage. This group of individuals are at such a disadvantage. If there's a possibility to have a forty-hour work week to include health benefits or employee benefits, then that would be helpful, but that is not the reality.

They are not promised work tomorrow. By that I mean, a patient who is well today may not be tomorrow morning. If this is the case, the HHA will not meet their patient the next day, which means they will not have income that day. Their next assignment is not promised. They are not paid for hours not worked nor is there any compensation for the loss of scheduled time.

This type of employment makes meeting their financial needs difficult to impossible. It is the type of employment that cannot promise healthcare or full-time salary benefits for the caregivers who are maintaining the longevity of the elderly population.

Financial Strain of the HHA

The HHA has a responsibility to their own family. Many are immigrants to this country and are not eligible for public assistance, but they are willing and capable of learning to become a certified HHA, as it may apply appropriately to that state. Some states do not require the training of a certified HHA, lowering the standards of practice overall of the HHA profession. The home care programs in all fifty states need to meet the same curriculum and board of nursing requirements no matter which state the member resides in.

Many of the HHAs must work around school schedules of their young children. With an average hourly rate of $12 per hour, the HHA faces many obstacles and finds it very difficult to meet their personal and household needs. However, it does prepare them for the ability to obtain disability benefits and social security benefits upon retirement.

Currently, many of these agencies do not pay for healthcare benefits. As it stands now, HHAs are required to maintain a minimum of thirty-three hours per week to be eligible to receive health benefits. The other obstacle is being able to afford such health benefits for themselves and their family. Some may be eligible for public assistance or Medicaid benefits, but for the most part, due to non-citizenship, they are not.

Few Benefits

Many HHAs are not provided paid time off, forcing them to go to work even if they are sick. They also have numerous unpaid holidays. A 401k plan is available only for full-time HHAs, but unfortunately, full-time status is very difficult to maintain. The member's continued services are unpredictable for an income-producing work schedule.

Some weeks, HHAs are not able to accumulate forty hours due to members being hospitalized, members taking a vacation, or personal time off requested by the HHA. The HHA is at the mercy of the agency to fill in the gap, which is unlikely. These factors create a major strain on the lives of HHAs, who feel abandoned by the administration.

Many HHAs also must work weekends in order to make ends meet. Some will work for other agencies when more income is needed but not available at their current agency. A weekend shift differential is another benefit unacknowledged. Unfortunately, time spent traveling between members is also not covered. A forty-hour week for an individual in another industry would be a fifty-hour week for the HHA due to the travel time.

The Need for Representation

HHAs require the voice or representation of an organization outside of their employer's scope of practice. Reporting their concerns to corporate compliance, even anonymously, is not utilized by the HHA because of the fear of retaliation. Many just do not trust the compliance officer.

HHAs feel abandoned, as if they are merely a means to an end for a business. Many feel mentally shackled by an industry that only recognizes them as a payroll ID or number on a check, rather than a human being often carrying the weight of a family on their shoulders.

Humiliation/Lack of Respect

Many HHAs experience humiliation such as verbal abuse and even sexual abuse by the members they are there to help. The Medicaid population is considered to be those individuals who live below the poverty line.

The HHA needs to be respected because they are one of the few people who take care of our elderly population. They come with a willing heart to deliver their best care for their member's lifestyle and well-being; however, they often go home with bittersweet feelings due to the trials and tribulations of the day. These challenges often stem from patients' home environments that are not always favorable.

Their resilience and commitment to get to their patients and to care for them is something that needs to be honored. Instead, persistent humiliation is accepted by the authorities managing the home health agencies. HHAs want to be respected because of their humility for the profession of home care. Conversely, many have a negative experience such as frequent humiliation from the home health agency management team and members.

Humiliation experienced by the HHA has been commonly reported yet met with minimal support of the contracted home health agency.

Early on in my career as an HHA supervisor, I trained on the job as I traveled from home to home. Prior to this, I had minimal experience by which to compare. The RN would create a plan of care according to the member's needs by assessing the member's general health history and medication, the home environment, and the ability of the HHA to be safe in a member's home.

High Need, Low Retention

The United States is spending billions of dollars on home care, according to the Center for Medicare and Medicaid Services. There is overall concern of a growth of forty-one percent from 2016. This appears to be the reason for the increased job opportunities for those who can meet the supply and demand of the home care industry. Yet there are unfortunate circumstances in retaining these care workers.

There are other overlooked issues where home healthcare workers do not have the organizational support of their employers to voice their concerns. The RN, such as I, will do everything possible to represent the HHA's concerns, and issues confronted in patients' homes in a nonunionized state. I have presented evidence as an advocate for the HHA. These HHAs are trained and now have expertise in home care; however, it is hard to succeed in an industry that is poorly managed.

Yielding to the Pressures

The initial assessment approving the care is begun by the RN assessor representing the HMO, who will commit to the member needing or not needing home health services. The RN's assessment is completed with the implementation of a plan of care. The member consents to the RN's plan of care.

The plan of care is used by the HHA to help guide the daily requirements of personal care. This plan is a standardized legal document required by the Medicaid standards of practice and completed by the RN. The HHA must make sure daily activities are completed and signed by the member.

In most scenarios, the member will admit to needing assistance with personal care. However, occasionally an uninformed member will admit to not needing any personal care services but will need housekeeping services. The nurse assessor will document the findings to be reported to the director of nurses or assigned team leaders. These findings are then reported to the HMO assigned to the member, who initially approved the contract for the assigned hours.

Numerous cases of members not needing personal care but wanting housekeeping will go undisclosed because the members are not informed of the regulations, or they have little concern for abiding by the regulations as it applies to the Medicaid-approved home care services. The HHA will eventually yield to the abnormal pressures of their financial needs and become the enabler, silent in their observations, because of the need to keep working. In turn, they will embrace whatever it takes to bring home that weekly salary.

Remember, the HHA is approved by Medicaid standards to deliver personal care as a priority to the payment plan. There are a few people who will disclose the wrongdoing and not endorse a member with fraudulent intent who accepted the Medicaid/HMO's approval of contract. This whistleblowing certainly does not come without a price to pay.

Exposing members will result in the loss of revenue for the agency. The honest HHA will now have to wonder if they will ever get another assignment. They must wonder if because they are doing the right thing, do they overlook the evil that will continue, or should they stand for righteousness?

Unsafe Conditions

I've been disillusioned by many working conditions accepted by the HHA. There are homes with bugs and rodent infestations, health hazards, drug use, unsafe buildings, and stairwell conditions with nonworking elevators. I've entered private pay homes and was able to detect fear and deep concern in the HHA, or there was a sense of distrust expressed by the HHA.

Upon doing a home assessment, the RN may see the home environment is not safe for the HHA, and it can be a liability to the agency as well as for themself. In many cases, the HHA must adjust to working in these conditions to get paid. Sadly, the HHA is used to working in these environments. To prevent loss of revenues, one certain agency requires five incidents where there is verbal abuse of a patient to a staff member—primarily HHAs—before a cancellation or reporting of services is given to the member's health provider.

I am highly concerned about the disgrace the HHA must endure. This makes me wonder how many providers (agency owners) and their office personnel have ever been into the inner-city apartments with an HHA attending to the Medicaid recipients.

While in search of the truth, we must also evaluate two important questions:

1. How is this affecting the mental and physical health of the HHA?
2. If the HHA doesn't do this work, then who will take care of the elderly, who rightfully require assistance?

The patients who are older and frail require the home care services of an HHA. Taking care of our HHAs, in the important role they play of providing optimum healthcare to elderly patients, is vital to the outcome of the current pandemic. We can either pay close attention to these matters and concerns or be faced with the consequence of the elderly inundating the hospitals. Healthcare workers are already at risk and due to pandemics like COVID-19, there is limited availability of HHAs.

HHAs need representation. The HHA requires the support of the governing body in the following areas:

- to have representation of their concerns (HHA unions and associations do not exist.)

- to recognize the HHA as the liaison between doctor, community, and patient
- to maintain and report, without punishment, the adherence of the Medicaid guidelines by the patient, HHA, and the home health agency alike
- for the HHA to be allowed to report to an organization of the state when services are not required (For example: hotlines or telephone numbers to protect the identity of the HHA or others)

Some of the concerns of the HHAs are:

- hourly rate increase per patient needs and classification of care
- paid benefits to be recognized
- job description of HHA as required by the Board of Nursing (currently only recognized in some states)
- reporting of their concerns as it relates to patients
- knowing and feeling that their lives matter
- representation outside of the hiring agency
- recognition of their profession
- rewards for their efforts
- incentives for continued education

CHAPTER FIVE

OUR HEALTH MATTERS

Blindsided

The home health agencies do not identify with what it is like for an HHA to go into a home unescorted. COVID-19 brought a fast and challenging awakening to the healthcare industry. In the middle of all that, we saw HHAs, who were regularly and bravely on the front line of patient home care, be forgotten.

COVID-19 was identified in January 2020. There was very little said about it up until March 14, 2020, as it related to the HHA or any other healthcare worker who entered a member's home or senior living facility. The home health agency received minimal education on prevention or recognizing potential contamination in a member's home. Many elderly people simply do not have the social support required to keep them free of contamination. As the health professionals declared, the elderly were the most vulnerable in contracting the virus.

A great fear of the unknown was evident. The HHAs had no one to turn to for knowledge on how to keep from being contaminated. The media covered all the healthcare workers who could be exposed to this virus if the proper personal protective equipment (PPE) such as masks, gloves, gowns, and facial shields weren't in place. The media wasn't considering the "other" healthcare workers, the HHA, who primarily took care of the elderly and disabled individuals in the privacy of their homes.

Once again, it was up to the field RN to allay the patient's as well as the HHA's fears. Isolation and social distancing were the only things to do, and many chose to abandon their caregiver responsibilities. The elderly were locked behind their doors, and the only ones who could visit were the essential healthcare workers.

Lack of Education/Preparation

Many agencies were not prepared for this type of disaster. Before the pandemic, the agency did not see the need to teach the habit of frequently changing disposable gloves and the use of masks when the member simply displayed symptoms of upper respiratory discomfort. The barriers were taught during an orientation class but enforcing it would be costly for the company's finance department.

COVID-19 created yet another difficult situation for HHAs due to the lack of education because of concerns about bringing them together into a classroom, which left them feeling helpless. As the agency failed to give them answers, I then became inundated with "help me" phone calls from members, HHAs, and relatives alike.

The home health agencies were not prepared with the standard PPE. The regulations were not categorized or prioritized by importance. Home health agencies were chaotic and undersupplied with PPE. Very little information was given to the home care workers, and fear and anxiety in the patients and HHAs skyrocketed.

The agency failed to educate the HHAs and patients on the care expected during the pandemic. Members and HHAs were poorly instructed in the practice of social distancing and increased handwashing. Social distancing couldn't really apply to a patient's home. It's impractical. Given the working conditions and the care provided to the elderly, it is a wonder why these HHAs had to practically beg for the minimal PPE given to them. The HHAs were supplied with two masks for the entire week, regardless of the number of patients they were caring for.

The agencies certainly were not practicing standard precautions. As an employee of a health agency, I can speak to the lack of supplies given to both the HHAs and the nurses. A common response was that they were on backorder. Should they abandon their patient because they don't have the protective equipment to cover their face and hands? It is sad to say that the only thing protecting the patient from the aide and the aide from the patient was their prayers and faith to endure the overwhelming fear of a disease we knew too little of. What we did know was the outcome for the individual patients and HHAs was unknown but taking the lives of many human beings.

Patients were in fear about how contamination could be prevented in their homes. Their only reassurance was locking the door to the outside world. I was privileged to be assigned fifty Category 1 members who were bedbound or had a dependent with mental or physical disabilities.

Initially, there was little support given to the RN entering the many patients' homes throughout the pandemic. Many businesses worked from their homes where it was practical, including the home health agency I worked for. There was the receptionist and a filing person who were mandated to report to work every day for the purpose of servicing any HHA who needed PPE. There was no protective plan to minimize exposure to the RN field supervisor or the HHA. Full-time RNs did not have a choice except to put faith to work.

There were other healthcare industries such as medical offices and other home health agencies that did stop all unnecessary visits to limit the exposure of the community nurse. For the HHA, it meant the revenues of the business would decrease if they did not report to their assignment. The pandemic surfaced the truth and fraud spoken of in this book. Suddenly, the patients were declining their care to prevent the exposure from the individuals entering their home, especially since many continued to use public transportation.

This was a great opportunity for the home care agencies and HMO to assess the actual need for home care services whether there was a pandemic or not. The home care agency who employed the RN certainly did not have a disaster plan in place. I spoke to the representative of the accreditation who admitted they were adjusting as the Centers for Disease Control (CDC) guidelines were provided.

Once again, I was left with no answers and an agency that was also waiting on the CDC guidelines. For the HHA, business must go on because patients must be seen every sixty days or more frequently, as per the Medicaid guidelines. In April 2020, the directive would allow the nurse to see the member but only if the member allowed. Many members greatly feared what COVID-19 could do, especially to the older community.

The HMO stopped all RN visits and only continued on-site visits for new members or those where an MD noted a change in status and requested an increase in the awarded hours needed. I spoke to other RNs in the home healthcare industry. I, along with many RN field nurses, felt forgotten in the healthcare system. There was no one to turn to for support. The one thing that was certain was the poor planning for the pandemic of 2020.

Difficult to Impossible Circumstances

A fellow nurse worked for another large agency. We both worked in Newark, New Jersey, a highly populated area. It was reported to have many hot spots, which meant a high percentage of individuals with COVID-19 and an escalating number of deaths were reported. We both worked many miles from the offices or our homes. It was heartbreaking. The pandemic changed the course for many in the field.

Many HHAs will admit that needing to use the restroom sometimes meant having to go outside the member's home and to a nearby restaurant or even back to their own home. Others used judgment as to who else lived in the home and cooperated with the CDC guidelines. It was especially disheartening when a fellow nurse admitted that the use of a restroom was a portable potty in the back seat of her car. Please keep in mind that we were working in a deeply underprivileged area and not a fancy suburb. My heart ached for this nurse who needed to support her family and continue to meet the six patients per day the agency demanded of her. Meeting our elimination necessities became a health hazard as the public restrooms were closed.

Once again, the CDC guidelines exposed the lives of many healthcare workers entering the homes of many who did not need services. The care was rightfully delivered by the essential caregivers to those members who met Category 1 or 2. These members of Category 1 or 2 needed meal preparation, bathing, or were bed bound.

The fear of the legal implications and the financial interest unnecessarily exposed many healthcare workers to COVID-19. Compliance, as we understood later in the year and approved by the Medicaid administration, was to do as many telephone monitoring visits as possible. The RN, with the direction and guidance of the administrative staff, would see members in their homes when necessary. On March 30, 2020, I was assigned to see a patient for a return to service assessment. I had the advantage of knowing this member. With a telephone assessment, I established that the member was capable of remaining independent in all ADL. For two months, he was independently caring for himself.

The proper screening of this kind of evaluation, when it comes to the home care agencies and the field nurses, had not been examined enough to prevent unnecessary spread of COVID-19. RNs and HHAs are considered essential workers and are expected to be ethically and professionally correct. The call of duty should not compromise the health status of a member or the health of the healthcare employees.

The response by the health agency's administration was that many of the HHAs lived in the same hot spots. The HHA was living in fear, and the leaders would not provide emotional and educational support needed by the essential home health caregivers.

It was with great effort that a nurse turned to the resources recommended on the Internet and the Department of Health, if and when they answered the phone calls. Little direction was given to the HHAs, and supplies were limited and on back order for several weeks. Many of the HHAs did not have a means of transportation for getting to an office many miles away from their patient's home. When the effort was made, they were given five pairs of gloves and two facial masks for the week.

They expressed a feeling of fear and abandonment. Many needed spiritual support to get through the first few months of the pandemic. Many contracted COVID-19 and others graduated to heaven. Educating and giving spiritual support became my number one priority. I encouraged them to reach out to me at any time. When they were unable to obtain their supplies, I delivered the PPE (gloves, gowns, mask, sanitizing gel) required by the Occupational Safety and Health Administration. It was imperative, having stressed the importance of frequent handwashing and the use of the PPE, that they report any signs of illness at a member's home.

Of course, this did not guarantee the individual would not contract the virus. Prevention was and is a key factor. The HHAs were informed of their own risk. There may be more than one individual in the home who may not comply with the cross-contamination policy, decline the use of a mask where required, and not be compliant with social distancing.

The HHA did not have a sufficient supply of the protective gear needed to prevent contamination, such as masks, gowns, gloves, and head caps. Healthcare workers are very much prone to contamination due to their close contact with patients. I especially speak of the HHA, who I continued to educate on the symptoms to report, such as fever, cough, shortness of breath, and fatigue.

Many of our elderly are already medically compromised. We must keep in mind the HHAs are nonmedical personnel and are likely to see the symptoms as chronic everyday discomforts, such as those individuals with chronic obstructive pulmonary disease, sinus or allergy conditions, and bronchial asthmatic diseases.

It is imperative to have a plan of action for the daily healthcare personnel both inside and outside of the hospital. I made many attempts regarding this in March of 2020. The Department of Health did not have a clue as to how to act on my question:

> *"Mr. Jason, the schools have closed, businesses have chosen to work remotely, and the hospitals have also taken precautions. What precautions have been taken to protect and also prevent the spread of COVID-19, as it relates to the HHAs attending to the elderly?"*

I made him aware that the home health agency barely supplied gloves and certainly did not have a supply of antibacterial gel, gowns, masks, or goggles.

> *"Will PPE be made available at all times regardless of the current events of the virus?"*

Mr. Jason could only answer questions relating to someone being a carrier of the virus. He did not have the name or department within the Department of Health to refer my concern to. It was just another dead end as to who would be the voice for the silent, unrepresented HHA. The HHA was dealt unmerited suffering, which I can attest to, as I made calls to our agencies myself in hopes of getting assistance with the proper PPE supplies that the HHA required. Many HHAs were denied entry to their clients' homes due to the lack of these supplies, which should have been supplied by the agencies.

Eventually, the HHA and other medical professionals were allowed to enter the homes, but the relatives were left to see their loved ones from the window. The field RN and the HHA were a totally forgotten group of highly needed health professionals. These professionals remained on the frontlines for the sake of the home care agency. This was a very dark period for the HHA because taking care of a member meant leaving their own family with another caregiver because the schools, like other industries, were shut down.

I mentioned to Mr. Jason my concern that every agency should identify and separate which members were living alone and required assistance along with those who required food preparation or the purchase of food. The HHA, with proper screening of the RN case manager and field RN, can identify which member can temporarily meet their daily needs and prevent the risk of any cross-contamination.

Many of the patients may live with other individuals who may not abide by the rules of prevention and infection control, putting the HHA at higher risk. The HHA may lack the knowledge or resources to understand a health crisis. Many were told they are negligent if they do not report to their patient assignment. Without the proper education and PPE, they would be putting themselves at risk. There were no monetary incentives for their efforts, and it certainly was not one of recognition either. Just to make a point, the HHA was getting paid $11 per hour. There was hope the rate would be $12 per hour by the end of the year 2020. The average rate today is $12-$14 per hour.

If health professionals become ill, the outcome is not good for anyone's morale or physical support. The care rendered to patients in the home are not as controlled as those which you would find in a hospital. HHAs are currently given the bare minimum of PPE. Currently, they are sent into the workplace with the one pair of gloves per patient each day.

Preventative medicine cannot be practiced with shortcuts. That will eventually hurt the same helping hands that are serving the members in their homes. The risk of compromising, whether to identify those members requiring daily assistance verses those members who are only in need of light housekeeping, should not be the reason an HHA resumes an assignment and risks contamination of themself and others.

An HHA can quickly report the signs and symptoms of a probable case of COVID-19 until specimens can be confirmed by the laboratory. Lack of the necessary precautions can put the HHA worker and community nurse at risk. The plan is to keep the contamination to a minimum. Education and reporting of the home environment are done by the field nurse and the HHA about the possibility of contracting COVID-19 and the potential absence of employees. The HHA is a growing population of healthcare workers. Most are unable to afford healthcare. The healthcare agencies were providing little or no support other than the gloves and mask that were minimally supplied.

The HHAs have families of their own and preventing contamination with the proper working gear can prevent contamination from the patient to the home health worker or from the worker to the patient.

As the RN entering the patient's home, it is difficult to understand why the healthcare agencies have not increased their level of precautions. This is not to be taken lightly because it applies to the health of these workers. Many of our HHAs will go on to assist patients to prevent payroll deduction or loss.

Keeping Quiet

The dangers surrounding the HHA have been evident, but much will go undisclosed. Many HHAs will even avoid discussing the dangers to prevent the loss of their employment. For example, until the pandemic, HHAs were not given masks, gloves, or gowns needed to protect themselves from exposure or contamination. The HHAs are basically keeping many of the older population from being admitted into the hospitals, and they are helping members remain in the comfort of their homes.

The HHAs are not nurses and are not trained to assess and make any medical nursing judgments based on their findings. They are required to report any change in the member's overall condition at any time. This supports the reason nurses are needed to make the required calls and visits to the patient's home to identify the potential of any imminent changes in the member's health. The HHA does not have the knowledge to foresee a change in their member's health, but they will have an inclination and with guidance and confidence from the assigned RN, unnecessary hospitalization can be avoided.

I believe it's a requirement in the responsibility of the home health agency to assess the health status of both the HHA and the patient. This is a critical time in global health issues. There are many elderly and disabled who are autoimmune compromised. That leaves a home health worker exposed to potential contaminants that are not yet showing evidence of disease, putting both the patient and the HHA at risk.

This has been experienced with the usual cold and flu season. Healthcare workers must be allowed to report the infirmity when symptoms have developed. This model of care can prevent medical symptoms from being prolonged without treatment. Early intervention will prevent complications of unstable health issues leading to hospitalization and premature death in the frail, elderly population.

Failure to identify an unsafe environment prior to the start of an assignment has been a Medicaid protocol reinforced by the accreditation. It is unfortunate when the RN has not been adhering to the protocol. The member's environment is initially assessed by the HMO RN assessor, who then finalizes the denial or approval of the Medicaid award for services in a contract.

The assigned home health agency will provide the type of care the member requires. However, the contract does not indicate an environmental analysis as is required by the home health agency's RN assessor advising the home care agency of any unhealthy or unsafe concerns. This is vital to the home healthcare worker to be able to safely enter the member's home. In many private home health agencies, personnel will visit the patient prior to assigning the HHA to the patient. This practice will prevent liability issues with unsafe environments.

The pre-assignment visit for the liability of the caregivers and visiting nurses is not paid to the agency by the HMO. Therefore, it is not cost effective to the Medicare provider. The private home care agency will incorporate the charge into the contract. The probable loss to the private care agency is the contract occurrence if the client disagrees with the agency's pre-assignment visit.

There is failure of the RN's assessment by the Medicaid HMO to report to the requesting agency an unsafe environment. We have a responsibility to the HHA to provide them with a safe and healthy work environment. We should not be putting the lives of healthcare professionals in the hands of a member whose living conditions are not considered safe and healthy.

Why do nurses and HHA accept work under such horrific conditions? The HHA, for example, may have limited choices. The inability to apply any other learned skills will inhibit the HHA from wisely choosing appropriate locations.

The fact that the elderly are living longer does not necessarily mean that an HHA would have to risk personal health and well-being for the sake of accepting a patient care contract. The location where the HHA is providing care to the elderly person should be investigated and the environmental assessment completed. The assessment should ascertain whether the member's environment is a safe place for the HHA to care for them in.

Some of the concerns I have encountered during my RN visits are related to the location, the patient's home environment and living conditions, disruptive family members, and rodents. It is an understandable concern to have the elderly living in an unhealthy and unkept environment.

It is the healthcare professional's responsibility to report an elderly person's unsafe living conditions to Adult Protective Services. For disabled, elderly individuals, the HHA may be their only source of survival and health maintenance. As healthcare providers in the home care industry, it is imperative that the healthcare motives also make a difference in the lives of the HHA. We can make safe and healthy choices and report to the appropriate individuals who can assist with making a healthy and safe decision for the members and caregivers.

The decisions of home care and the health of the older population are the responsibilities of the healthcare professionals. There are other reasons why an unhealthy home environment may go unreported. This is very common but not spoken about so the agency can maintain a business and the HHA can continue to make an income. This is by no means ethically or professionally correct for the physical and mental well-being of the HHAs.

The home care industry must make better choices as to where and how an HHA must tolerant their working conditions. I've personally gone to visit a patient and knew very well the HHA would not be safe in that environment. The HHA would certainly agree with me, but the concern would be, "I cannot afford to *not* have this patient."

It was my responsibility to discontinue the services due to the unsafe conditions for an employee. It was fortunate the member was independent with their ADL and certainly did not require home care services. This was one of many cases that influenced me to be the active voice for the HHA and one where a corrective action plan was needed for a safe and healthy outcome regarding workplace negligence overlooked by the HMO and the home care agency's administration. In acknowledgement to the HHA who may approve working in an unsafe or unhealthy environment, the RN representing the agency has the ultimate authority to discontinue services to prevent any cause for liabilities.

While the numbers are unclear due to fear of reporting, some HHAs have privately confessed to being verbally and sexually abused by members. The HHA is not typically respected for the types of skills they have. It is the responsibility of the home healthcare agency to show compassion and respect to the HHA. Many HHAs go beyond their scope of practice to have a relationship with the patient that results in improvement and stability of the patient's health.

The HHA must develop a genuine relationship with their supervisor as well as the agency's personnel for optimum patient and employee satisfaction. The HHA has a narrow choice of selection in the home care industry. The choices are whether to accept a bedbound member verses a non-bedbound member.

HHAs and RNs visiting the homes have experienced many of the rewards their visits bring to the once deteriorating individual. They are also faced with the many oppositions that rural areas bring, such as diseases, drug abuse, rodents, and general unclean living conditions. Then there are the unsafe living conditions many employees face every day.

Many agencies talk about providing an escort service for nursing personnel, yet I have not seen this once in my twenty years of practice. There were assignments, as the RN supervisor, I would decline due to the location of the assignment being dangerous to employees. The shortage of field nurses evidently increased due to the pandemic, reflecting the inability of the home care agency to remain accountable to the regulations required to meet the increased demand of the patient-to-nurse ratio.

There are choices for the RN. In my case, being bilingual, I was viewed as the lifesaver. I was able to cover a larger group of individuals, yet I didn't receive respect or proper compensation.

This type of employment is certainly the survival of the fittest for both the HHA and the RN. The RN will, at a minimum, enter twenty-five different homes per week, and the HHA may have one to two homes per day or week, depending on the schedule. The meek nurse cannot survive. As the RN, you must put on your combat boots, and your fighting goal is to come out without incident. When I told my supervisors about the unsafe observations, the administration would respond with, "welcome to home care."

I stayed in the home care industry with the hope of sharing my experience and exposing the abuse of HHAs and RNs with the administration, Board of Nursing, and the accreditation associated with the agency. I did not want to be just another voice of experience but instead be the voice that would be heard.

The home care agency I worked with has not been able to maintain the employment of RNs. I originally, like a previous colleague, did not choose to work in the poverty-stricken areas due to unsafe and unhealthy working conditions. I contracted to work at the safer and healthier areas of Northern New Jersey. However, I chose to return to the unsafe areas so others might know about them.

CHAPTER SIX

FRAUD AWARENESS AND DOCUMENTATION

During the many years of my nursing career, I have not seen a greater need than the representation for HHAs and the ethical role in the care of the elderly and disabled adults. There was certainly a rise of tension and unrest in my well-being and spirit that deserved my intervention. It is for this reason this book came into being.

There were years when it was my utmost intention to shed light on this very common but unspoken concern in the home care industry as it applies to home care HHAs and field nurses alike. It is important to educate the public on the fraud being committed by the individuals employed by the Medicaid, fee-for-service, and home health agencies. The HHAs, supporting office staff, and RN employees have little to no administrative knowledge to support the initial or continued approval of the Medicaid fee-for-service home care services.

Here are a few of the ways fraud is committed in the industry.

Member Fraud

The RN will perform an assessment based on observation and a general history, and they will score the assessment. I've done this type of assessment and can speak from experience, not speculation. The tool used for the assessments are statements used in a format of questions to the individual. Unfortunately, not everyone is honest in the assessment.

The individual responds to several questions, such as, "Do you require assistance with bathing?" The response can be any version of the following:

- "No, I do not need assistance with bathing."
- "No, I do not need assistance from anyone; my family member will help me with bathing."
- "I prefer to take care of my personal needs myself."
- "I do not need these services to take care of my personal needs."

The RN case manager will conclude this portion of the assessment at a score of zero, based on the responses. This member should not receive an award of service. Members must meet at least one of the criteria, which is at a minimum one hands-on activity, such as bathing, transferring, or assistance with ambulation. Members are made aware that Medicaid services, when approved, will require the home care agency to adhere to the Medicaid regulations related to ADL only.

Medicaid recipients have been known to be approved by making statements such as:

- "I cannot bathe myself."
- "I need assistance with bathing."
- "I need help with meal preparation."
- "I am unable to walk into the bathtub."
- "I am unable to change positions or bend."

These statements should be aligned with the findings observed by the RN assessor. Currently, the Patient Care Assessment tool used by the RN is just a form with twenty questions, requesting a response from the Medicaid recipient. When the denial of services is sent to the member, the member knows they can simply transfer to another Medicaid-approved health insurance provider, which will likely result in approval.

This is another disparity within the Medicaid requirements, whereas the regulations do not require the individual HMO to do an in-depth search of the resident's history and reasons for past approvals or denials on record. If this search was required, residents would not be approved when previously denied, unless correctly substantiated. As the owner of an agency, I began to see how many agencies had to choose to stay or not stay in business. What often kept an agency in business was the manipulation of both Medicaid and the agency.

Role Play

Many of the members are educated on the presentation that the RN assessor gives at the member's home. Therefore, the member is prepared to role play difficulties with the ADL. The RN may have excellent intuition; however, they are liable if their recommendations are contrary to the observations. A hands-on assessment, like the one done in a medical facility or medical office, will prevent fraudulent presentations by the member.

The RN assigned by the agency will prepare to complete a physical assessment for the member along with a master plan of care to help guide the HHA with the ADL. The member is already approved the hours and will continue to demonstrate their need for assistance with the ADL. In most cases, the inconsistencies commenced immediately, probably due to inappropriately assigned awards of services.

A member who may have evidence of deficiencies with ambulation, transferring, bathing, and limited mobility of the upper and lower limbs may, without question, need the assistance required with their ADL, as the guidelines mentioned. The activities requiring assistance must be visual, measurable, and the limitations in the skills highly evident. When these skills are not evident to the agency RN field supervisor, there is supposed to be a reporting mechanism funneled directly to the director of nurses, who reports the findings and inadequacies to the health insurance provider (HMO).

The inadequacies are against the small percentage of personnel who will do the right thing, in spite of losing employment. The gathering of information for this book took several years of my old mistakes and wondering how the agencies continue to ignore the false impersonations in most of the member's homes.

Who Is Responsible?

It is a known fact that the home healthcare system in the United States is in crisis as we approach a shortage of healthcare workers. Training, hiring, and maintaining the employee is a growing concern. The state funding at the Medicaid level and the services provided by the HHA, orchestrated primarily by the home healthcare agency, would need immediate attention regarding the HHA's job description, the hourly rate paid to the home health provider agency, and an ethically correct award of service hours per member.

The responsible party for adhering to the ethics set forth by the code N.J.A.C. 10:60-3.1 must be established. First and foremost, the healthcare provider assigning the award of service (e.g., United Healthcare, Amerigroup, Horizon NJ, WellCare, etc.) and the corresponding agency should ultimately be responsible for identifying false use of HHA services.

Some questions to consider:

- Who is responsible to report?
- What needs to be reported by the HHA? Verbal abuse—members have been known to verbally abuse the HHA in reference to their race, color, religion, or culture. Some are known to request only a particular race or culture.
- What needs to be reported by the Medicaid recipient?
- When personal care services are no longer needed.
- What needs to be reported by the RN upon entering the home? Environmental conditions, negligence of the patient's personal needs, abuse by the member or HHA, and danger to the well-being of the HHA.
- The need to cancel the HHA service—no personal care services required.
- Using Medicaid-approved hours for housekeeping services only
- Inability of the Medicaid recipient to care for themself independently after the HHA has completed their assignment. (Members have been left in a medical bed with the side rails up, awaiting the CHHA to arrive the next day—a case of negligence.)

The HMO has a responsibility to adhere to the N.J.A.C. 10:60-3:1-3.3. The chain of command begins with the doctor's order received from the member's private physician. Other health professionals, such as the RN, social worker, or a primary caregiver, may identify the need of HHA services in the areas of ADL (bathing, meal preparation, dressing, feeding, light housekeeping).

Insufficient or Incomplete Assessments

Personal care is the primary reason Medicaid pays for assistance and awards services. The other areas mentioned above (light housekeeping, meal preparation, shopping) also help with maintaining an optimum level of health for the member.

Fraudulent activity comes into play when the assessor fails to identify which of the physical needs requires assistance and bases their outcome on verbal responses as opposed to the physical examination of the activity. Asking a member if they are able to do their laundry and simply obtaining a "yes" or "no" response is quite different than observing a member having difficulty changing positions or using their upper and lower extremities. A visual assessment is not usually the case in many of the home assessments.

The RN completes the assessment as a representative of the HMO provider. The assessor takes a hypothetical guess that the member has a disability with the task of the laundry. It is not up to the assessor to determine whether or not the member meets the criteria for the award of hours for home care service. It is up to the assessor to be correct in their documentation and allow the MDs assigned to that healthcare provider the final review of the assessor's findings, then comments to be approved or disapproved.

The RN HMO assessor is identifying the individual in areas such as no assistance needed, supervision needed, limited assistance needed, extensive assistant needed, or total dependency on the caregiver.

In the Patient Care Assessment tool, the RN assessor may feel compelled to document that the member requires supervision or limited assistance. The question is not whether the member requires the use of a cane or walker to assist with ambulation and prevent falls, but is the member independent in their ADL? There are many non-Medicaid recipients who are cane or walker dependent, but with occupational therapy, they can be functional in their daily needs when it applies to light housekeeping.

Conflict of Interest

Let's look at the areas of bathing and transferring. Most accidents will happen in the patient's bathroom. This will be the major reason for a member requiring an award for service paid by Medicaid. Many times, the member requiring assistance with bathing is receptive to the assistance by the caregiver either because they have limitations with their gait or their transferring skills have deteriorated. This same member may usually require assistance with applying lotions and dressing, especially with garments of the lower limbs.

Someone whose health is deteriorating can be maintained in their home avoiding further deterioration and hospitalization, providing there are no other barriers or negligence beyond the job description of the HHA. In much of my experiences in the field, both as an RN assessor and a field supervisor for HHAs, there is much to be said and much more not said because of the limitations of an appropriate examination and physical skills assessment.

When hired, a nurse should have years of experience at different levels of the nursing profession due to the level of autonomy required to complete an assessment. Today, because of all the elements that field RNs confront, it is the reason I've seen a short retention of field RN case managers as required by the agency's standard of practice. I will explore more of the discrepancies facing the RN hired by the Medicaid-approved home health agency.

The RN assessor could not accurately provide an assessment due to limited face-to-face verbal interviews provided by the Medicaid regulations. With experience, the RN compiling information on the initial assessment can be more intuitive in their documentation. Again, the nurse will find themself scoring a member based on a verbal response.

I do recall an RN who visited a member from the Medicaid state office prior to the year 2011, when a patient was being denied the award of services because the nurse asked to see the member's transferring skills into the bathtub. The nurse was not required to request any kind of demonstration of skills to properly score the assessment, according to the Medicaid standards.

Why should there be such a limited tool that cannot examine a member's physical and mental ability? In my opinion, that is what makes this an inept and fraudulent tool, a tool that avoids the best outcome by not preventing fraudulent activity across the many home health agencies and health insurance providers.

The RN must guard their license and prevent themselves from being accused of speculation or a biased opinion. This is the reason so many of the assessments are providing the reviewing HMO MD results that eventually approve fraudulent use of home care services.

A more functional assessment tool would require a physical exam and a questionnaire completed by a healthcare professional—as an outside source, rather than a source under the employment of the health insurance provider, who also has an interest in gaining the member. HMOs and their representatives avoid losing a member by approving the number of weekly hours for the potential member at all cost.

Looking the Other Way

This is exactly why fraudulent activity continues to occur by many of the HMO and home health agencies. The home health agency can stop fraudulent activity but will refuse and deny the cause for reporting fraudulently assigned services to a member. The home health agency does not want to lose revenue, so they will continue to look the other way instead of being ethically and legally correct.

The description and comments on an assessment are limited to the differentiation of a member who is highly limited to the totally independent one. As the RN assessor, I could not prove the member was moderately to highly independent when the member simply answered my questions, contrary to my observation.

Simply using the current tool would limit the proper collection of data for the necessary improvement. The increased approval of Medicaid-awarded hours of service can be curtailed to only those members whose physical assessment align with an improved assessment tool.

As you may or may not know, Medicaid recipients are the largest group of members who apply for home care as a long-term care service. The health insurance provider approves the award of the hours.

Whose responsibility is it to report the fraudulent use of the hours?

The RN representing the health insurance provider is employed to assess the member's impairments, which may require assistance with ADL. The RN assessor is required to document only those tasks that meet the criteria for assistance. But as I mentioned before, many are ignorant to the numerous cases that are approved without meeting the criteria. This leads me to believe this standard of practice is business as usual.

I have been on both sides of this business. I've been the RN assessor, the business owner of a Medicaid-accredited home health agency for a health insurance provider, and I've also been the RN supervisor for an accredited home healthcare agency. The ball can stop rolling right at the very start if the RN assessor does not find any reason for personal care assistance.

I recall being informed that if a member has been awarded hours, I should do everything possible to maintain those hours. That was the directive I received from the director of nursing. This would allow a contract to continue being approved for the agency as well as for the health insurance provider. This is such bureaucracy, which I continually wrote off as "the state officials just don't care what our tax dollars are wastefully paying for."

No One Wants to Lose Business

In most cases, the final number reached in an assessment isolates the member's need down to the category of housekeeping assistance only. It appears Medicaid members are seeking service solely for housekeeping. I have educated many HHAs throughout the last fifteen to twenty years to only document assisted activities completed and assigned as written on a plan of care personalized for the individual.

What many HHAs will do is submit their activity sheets with the ADL (required by Medicaid standards of practice) as rendered, when in truth they were not. Exposing this to their employer would likely create loss of a member, the possibility of not being able to obtain another assignment, or loss of employment.

The employer may acknowledge the incident reported as a member receiving services. The expected outcome is hopefully the undeserved services would be reported by the home health agency to the HMO. In many cases, I have gone back to see the placement of a newly assigned HHA, who now will do the fraudulent documentation, and business continues as usual.

The ironic, probably unsuspected, area of the accreditation body is the one where the RN field supervisor, employed by the home health agency, never reviews the weekly activity report submitted to the agency for claim submission. The activity reports are reviewed by non-medical personnel with no understanding of the master care plan, customized to meet the member's short and long-term goals.

Many of the HHAs are aware that if they do not document ADL, they will lose that patient for employment. Others will tell me if they do not apply it to their activity sheets, it will be returned to them for completion. The reasoning is if the claim is submitted or audited without rendering ADL hands-on assistance, it will be considered an inappropriate claim submission of services.

This will require that the home health agency return any payment received for that member. However, the HHA would receive payment for their services, putting the home health agency at a loss of revenue.

Now, imagine how many times the HHA should report a member who requested assistance from the RN assessor. The HHA has firsthand information to submit to their reporting RN supervisor. The visits are conducted by an RN supervisor every sixty days or less if required. The RN will ask similar questions at every visit as it relates to hands-on personal care.

Too Little Care

When a member whose ambulation is assisted with a cane or with a contact guard as per observation, but in reality, the member is able to ambulate with the cane without assistance by the HHA, the HHA may be assigned three hours in that day. They may have to assist with transfer once during their three-hour shift, but there are twenty-four hours in a day. Therefore, why does a member need only partial supervision or cueing with assisted ambulation?

The member may require assistance with the transferring activity of a wheelchair with activities that require a contact guard. An RN assessor or RN supervisor should be ascertaining the balance of the care required throughout the twenty-four-hour period. If the member lives by themself, either the member is self-sufficient, or the RN is negligent of reporting a member who needs a nursing home placement to eliminate potential harm or injury to themself and further deterioration.

Adult Protective Services would create the report, which would involve the member, next of kin, and the agency's findings. It is evident that the Medicaid home health program can be assigned up to forty hours per week. This will require private caregivers to be available during the hours the HHA is not assigned. One would think there should be continuous monitoring or some level of supervision throughout the day by another caregiver. In most case scenarios, this is the expectation to prevent injury related to falls and hospitalizations.

Assistance with ambulation may require some level of a contact guard. If a contact guard is required, the RN (either assessor or field supervisor) is responsible for indicating how this level of assistance is required throughout the full day and who is meeting this need. The assessment tool needs to be formulated to identify these details to accurately measure the need for services. For the RN assessor, that should be the only criteria to approve services by Medicaid.

Who Reports Services Not Rendered?

False documentation on the HHA activity sheet is the root cause for an agency's citation and potential denial of accreditation certification. Documentation accepted by the HHA is the personal care that has been delivered (bathing, skin care, ambulation, meal preparation).

Whose responsibility is it to report activities that are not rendered by the HHA? The HHA is ultimately responsible for reporting to their supervisor. The HHA should say what they are actually doing every day and not fraudulently document what an agency expects in order to submit a claim for payment. Regrettably, the fear of not having income prevents many HHAs from coming forward with the actual care being rendered in a patient's home.

The HHAs have been taught in their certification course the policies and procedures as well as the legal and ethical aspects required to prevent future lawsuits and the importance of reporting those matters, which do not align with the scope of practice to the agency.

The HHA is aware that the renewal of their HHA certification (every two years) is dependent upon the code of ethics and conduct and the performance evaluation completed by human resources and the field RN supervisor. The scope of practice has been defined for the HHA. It is expected that the HHA will report the skill not being done for the patient. However, if every HHA came forward with what is actually happening with the Medicaid recipient falsely accepting home care services, their employment may no longer be available.

The HHA has been known to have minimal support from the agency, and it's the reason why many of the findings in the member's home go unreported. Many HHAs do not have the confidence or trust that the report will not be a charge against them.

Many HHAs live with condemnation and humiliation for their profession. The HHA needs to feel worthy of their job description and work with humility, not humiliation. After all, HHAs are the reason our elderly stay out of repeated hospitalizations. It is time that their job description is revisited, and their voices represented.

Fraudulent Documentation

The regulations are standards of practice written so the auditor representing the state or accreditation body can identify fraud in the patient's file. The main focus in this book is manipulated documentation. The fraud is due to the way the questions are presented by the HMO assessor. Home care approved by Medicaid requires, at the minimum, one hands-on personal care needs activity to be met per day. For the most part, the member will either refuse personal care from the HHA or will not admit the discrepancy to the agency's RN at the assessment required every two months.

The HHA will document that they performed activities that were not done for the sake of getting paid. I have taught several courses to HHAs, and many have obtained their certificate to practice as a HHA by the Board of Nursing. It was of high importance that they understood the protocols and the cause for when and how to report fraudulent use of the Medicaid award of hours of service.

The HHA will get the opportunity early on in their career to experience how the nurse will implement all the parts of the home care agency's policies and procedures and the importance of the rules and regulations that maintain an accredited home care agency. At the start of the services, both the member and the HHA are acknowledging the member's Bill of Rights; Advanced Directives; Agreement Contract, which identifies who is responsible for payment; and the master care plan, which delineates the personal care needed for the optimum level of care.

The rules are reinforced as frequently as needed but especially every six months or sooner when a new master care plan (as per Medicaid standards) must be implemented. There may or may not be changes to the patient's medical status. The primary rule is to not document what you have *not* done for the member.

Time and time again, the exact opposite can be discerned but not proven. It's for the simple reason that if it isn't documented then it simply means the member does not require the services for PCAs. As the nurse completing the assessment, I have also seen documenting in which services of personal care were administered, but all I can do is inquire if they were done. However, it may be evident through observation that the member exhibits the capacity to administer personal care safely and independently, thus disqualifying the member for the services approved by Medicaid regulations.

The HHAs do not have a voice, but as a whole, they are a community that quickly teaches each other how to make the business work for them. Many of the agencies are well aware of the strategies the HHAs practice. The agency will not try to challenge the corruptive industry either because:

- They do not have proof.
- The challenge of getting proof is too great.
- It will decrease their revenues when the truth is revealed.

The Medicaid HMO can either decrease or increase the current Medicaid award of hours of services. In many cases, the member will benefit from changing from an assigned HMO to another. I do not want to give the impression that a member does not have the right to change or get the best an HMO can offer. The question is, at what point is there a standard of practice in which a member is denied approval?

Are we intimidated by the possibility of us (the nurse or the HHA) having made an incorrect analysis of the member's ability? One cannot make a mistake like this. If any reasons were identified that would indicate a need for personal care assistance, it should be known that this member would not be able to meet their daily needs outside of the Medicaid award of service hours.

Needs Beyond the Max Award

Members with substantial needs are those who require services seven days a week. The maximum hours approved for them would be forty hours. That would provide a maximum of five to six hours per day. Logically, this member would require services before and after the HHA service hours. Either the member already lives with family who can continue with caregiving before and after the assigned hours, or this member cannot safely meet their daily needs at home independently without incident. The truth of the matter is this type of member is usually placed in a skilled nursing facility due to lack of supervision and assistance of a caregiver.

The other type of member will be one who has the mental ability to make decisions but does not have the independence with their motor skills as in an assisted gate, poor balance, or the inability to ambulate. This member may not require assistance with bathing or skin and hair care, but they may require assistance with meal preparation. The award for this patient would then be for meal preparation and light housekeeping.

It's unfortunate that many who are scoring this patient will also find a need to inadvertently approve the other personal care activities that are already being done independently. Due to the poor assessment skills and tools currently used and submitted to the home management organization assigned, the member appears to be dependent on the HHA for the ADLs.

No Cross Checks

Typically, the member asks me to add the personal care needs being met on the care plan. During my visit, I am required to supervise any one of the personal care needs done by the HHA. The HHA agency is aware that the RN will not be at a patient's home exactly when the patient is being bathed for various reasons; for example, the RN might be at another member's home at that time. This is common. You can attempt to schedule five to six patients in a day to see them during one of the personal skills required to meet the requirements for Medicaid approval.

The RN has a quota to meet for an agency because they're the employer and you are the employee. The RN must record the visit as completed and why they did or did not see the actual activity is irrelevant. There is no strategy other than we are dealing with human beings who have personal schedules for bathing, skin care, and assistance with dressing. Many, if not all, members will not allow anyone to see them bathing except maybe a family member or the HHA.

Requirements expected of the supervising RN are certainly unrealistic and unreachable due to the many other clients scheduled to be seen during the same day. This causes many RNs to choose between noncompliance or fraudulent reporting. The RN is at the mercy of the member's honor and integrity of what's required by the Medicaid standards of practice.

Some circumstances create compliance issues because of overscheduling, which needs a platform for the analysts to research. This data is as valuable to the integrity of the approval and continuity of the services as it is to the actual performance of the service. Some members become complacent, knowing the RN will document what they are told rather than what can or cannot be observed. This can be improved with a better assessment tool.

Another issue going on is members are not reporting HHA absences. This is an abuse of the system. It often cannot be proven because of what appears to be a business within the business. The member may feel obligated to be like the majority and not report. The members receiving a Medicaid-awarded service should no longer have the privilege of choosing how and when an employee reports to their assignment. However, it is obvious that a better system is required to monitor the entrance and exit of an HHA into the member's home. Currently, agencies have implemented the use of personal cell phones and technology to monitor the schedule of the HHA and their reporting to an assignment.

The member's home must have a phone line of some sort (either land or mobile) by which the employee must call in. This should be mandatory because today there isn't one member I visit who doesn't have a working telephone.

However, this also adds an opportunity for the member to call in as the employee and do the reporting themselves. It appears the best solution is to mandate all employees assigned to

Medicaid-awarded HHA service to have compatible cell phones, allowing the appropriate applications to monitor their location.

Monitoring the HHA's location upon reaching the member's home will curtail the fraudulent activity as it applies to reporting or not reporting on a timely basis. Currently, this is the best system I've seen implemented in my years of doing home care supervision and the one system that can correct the majority of fraudulent activity by the HHA as well as the member supporting the HHAs.

It is important we all start doing what is correct, whether it is the HHA code of ethics or the reporting of member services based on honesty and ethical standards of conduct.

Best Practices for the HHA

- to have compassion for the care of others
- to be non-judgmental
- to be able to esteem the elderly and disabled person
- to be humble, kind, and compassionate to others
- to deliver high-quality care
- to refrain from fraudulent activity
- to report any notable fraudulent activity
- to report changes in the member's condition
- to continue in-service education
- to maintain an optimum level of health
- to respect the rights of the client

- to keep patient information confidential
- to be nondiscriminatory
- to report an unsafe environment
- to report abuse or negligence of the elderly and disabled
- to have knowledge of the member's medical limitations

The Doctor's Role

As mentioned previously, home care services require a doctor's order to initiate the application process. The doctor may or may not understand the criteria required to receive the home care services. They are very much led by the member under their care. Patients may have a long list of major limitations when visiting their private doctors, but for the most part, they do not present those limitations during the home assessment.

There is certainly a combination of events occurring that contribute to fraudulent approvals. The MD must have a history of all findings that indicate the member does not have full range of motion to either upper or lower extremities. The member may also have limitations with assisted mobility or any other compromising health condition. With a physical assessment, the doctor can identify the member's deficiencies and how home care service can benefit the member.

There are many cases where a member is independent, but their physician will approve an order for evaluation for HHA services. The physician's order must be honored and submitted to the HMO. There is a misconception among some members where they believe if a member's physician submits a prescription to the HMO, it will be honored without discussion or evaluation.

The fact is the HMO's assigned physician has the ultimate responsibility to approve or disapprove the services. Many physicians have encountered angry members when they refused to honor a prescribed order for the home care services. This led to manipulation of award outcomes and members who would just transfer to another physician to obtain the services. Many doctors are aware that their orders are not in compliance with Medicaid regulations. A modified assessment tool identifying the limitations by demonstration can and will improve the fraudulent use and the unnecessary ordering of home care services by the physician.

Billing

The billing department is another area worthy of discussion. Managing the operations of a home health agency provided me with understanding of the integrity one must have when sending out claims. The billing employee is highly oblivious to the fraudulent claim submissions because they do not have any awareness of the master care plan or the services rendered. This can only be identified and confirmed by the nurse's documentation and the HHA's weekly activity sheet submission.

The HHA is supposed to report the member's independence accurately, appropriately, and honorably. However, the HHA is frequently encouraged to complete the patient's daily activity report to indicate the need for personal care. The assessment the nurse completes should be the billing statement. The nurse's notes are of little value since the billing department does not read them to identify the reasons for home care services as one would do in a medical record where the federal government is the payor.

The fraudulent billing of Medicaid can be corrected when claim submission entails details of the care approved and rendered. The documentation from the RN assessor, field RN, and HHA comes from different sources, and discrepancies will deny the healthcare agency payment.

There are only certain limitations the Medicaid-awarded services will approve. The Medicaid officials expect that every claim submitted has followed Medicaid protocols. The claim submissions personnel should know how to access whether the information presented follows the protocol necessary for nonfraudulent claim submission.

Instead, without much investigation, the billing personnel simply complete and submit a claim based on the number of hours worked by an individual. Usually, the billing department will get summaries of the number of hours to be billed. There is no system in place that I know of that looks at the nurse's notes and identifies where the limitations are as they apply to that member's assisted ADL.

Integrity and Ethics

There is a major reason for continuation of approved home healthcare paid for by the Medicaid-approved award of hours.

There is a lack of information and policy education provided to the RN of the assigned home healthcare agency.

Every RN, either from an HMO or from an accredited home health agency, should look at their daily assignment with integrity. Florence Nightingale was the greatest nurse of all times and the founder of modern nursing. The RN's goal is to adhere to the Code of Ethics and the Florence Nightingale Pledge quoted by many nurses at graduation.

FLORENCE NIGHTINGALE PLEDGE

I solemnly pledge myself before God and in the presence of this assembly, to pass my life in purity and to practice my profession faithfully. I will abstain from whatever is deleterious and mischievous and will not take or knowingly administer any harmful drug.

I will do all in my power to maintain and elevate the standard of my profession and will hold in confidence all personal matters committed to my keeping, and all family affairs coming to my knowledge in the practice of my calling. With loyalty will I endeavor to aid the physician in his work, and as a 'missioner of health' I will dedicate myself to devoted service to human welfare.[4]

In the Interest of the Future

The Medicaid organizations must also step up to the standards of practice because they also have a responsibility to the charges they review annually or as they may apply to claim submission requirements. We rely on the accreditation organization to evaluate all the parts required by the standard of practice for one hundred percent compliance.

Legal standards of practice state if it wasn't documented, it wasn't done. And if it wasn't done, that agency should not get paid. We as citizens of the United States must take an interest in the future of the home care services made available to all elderly and disabled Americans needing assistance to maintain an optimum level of health daily.

Slippery Slope of Scope

The HHA's observation of the member's dependent and independent skills—meal prep, toileting assistance, ambulation, light housekeeping—is required for continuity of the Medicaid award of services. The HHA is not allowed to perform certain services not approved by the Medicaid award of assigned services. The HHA is not allowed to drive patients in their cars. They are also not allowed to administer medication or perform heavy housekeeping duties.

However, there is a majority of elderly, both Medicaid and Medicare recipients, who do require assistance with these tasks in order to maintain an optimum level of health. Many may have short or long-term memory loss and are unable to recall their schedule of medication or other events such as medical follow-up appointments.

There's also the individual who does not have significant others to assist with these very important ADL. Thus, this leaves the HHA to do the unscheduled, unapproved activities to maintain the health of the patient.

Meal preparation is also a very high concern for many of the elderly. As we are aware, the elderly may consume one meal a day if assisted. Assisting with one meal per day is important, but what about for the patient who needs two and three meals a day?

Medication Administration and Communication

The same is also true for medication administration. The HHA must be able to know the five "rights of medication" administration: right patient, right dose, right route, right drug, and right time. Right documentation has been added recently.

The HHA is required to have some general knowledge of adverse drug reactions. It is the role of the RN field supervisor to ascertain the level of understanding and literacy competency the HHA demonstrates. If the HHA can only speak minimal English, it would be difficult for them to both communicate with the member and to read the member's medicine labels. It is important that we take the matters of medication administration very seriously. The patient's needs are dependent on the HHA's knowledge and observation.

There is an awareness acknowledged by the RN who visits the members on a bimonthly basis as required by the Medicaid standard of practice. The HHA is already practicing medication administration without approval. As per the Board of Nursing, only a licensed RN can administer medication. The only other options would an approved medication certification or a medication administration program provided to the HHA.

Nurses were being trained via a continuing education program to facilitate where an HHA is delegated these duties on a case-by-case assessment. The home healthcare agency will need a medication aide training program approved by the New Jersey Department of Health and Senior Services, and the HHA also must pass the New Jersey Assisted Living Certified Medication Aide Exam—these are specific to New Jersey residents. The HHA can then attain the title of certified medication aide.

Many of the HHAs will find themselves assisting with medications due to the inability of the caregivers, if any. All HHAs who are trained have been certified and are aware of the Board of Nursing rules for medication administration. Certified HHAs who are not certified medication aides are not allowed to administer medications.

The HHA can remind the member to take their medication, but they are not able to assist with the pouring of the medication or assist in the preparation of the pill box. The HHA is aware of the importance of the member's medication schedule to maintain optimum health; therefore, they will assist the member with their medication with the hope of not having the matter disclosed to the supervisors or the home health agency. The HHA will constantly put themself at risk to maintain their credibility with the member and continued employment.

The RN can identify if there is a reason why a member cannot assist themselves with their medication and request a family member or significant other to prepare the pill box. However, there are many elderly people who do not have a significant other to help with that task. The only person they will see is a certified HHA.

The HHA who also acquires the medication administration certificate will be better prepared and profiled to assist that group of individuals with mental and physical disabilities in the process of taking their medicine or applying ointments.

The HHA is very much aware of those situations in a patient's home that can deny the member continued services. They fear reporting an issue against the member for the sake of their employment.

HHAs are to report conditions such as inability to recall medication schedules, inability to administer medication, increased Independence in personal care, or reluctancy to receive personal care.

Some of the fears associated with reporting the inability of a member to administer their own medication are losing the member as a client, a potential risk of danger to the member, and the probable need for skilled nursing facility placement. Adult Protective Services may have to be notified when all measures are exhausted, and the RN is absolutely certain the member is not capable of safely self-administering medication or making other decisions requiring stable mental ability to function without incident.

The nurse will pursue to locate another form of medication preparation for this individual. Calls to the member's family to assist in the task will also be encouraged. Fortunately, several pharmacies are packaging medications for daily administration. However, the member must be able to read and understand the medication label for route, dosage, and schedule. The primary goal is to safely maintain the elderly in their home environment and prevent unplanned hospitalization or nursing home placement.

The communication between the patient, primary caregiver, and the HHA is essential to maintaining a productive work environment and continuity of care. The home care service needs to meet the primary individual's needs to maintain an optimum level of health, medication preparation, shopping, medical follow-up, feeding, bathing, and assistance with gait and transfer.

Calling patients and reminding them of their medication schedule can be a more cost-effective approach. Pharmacies are now packaging the medication individually with color coding to indicate when the medication is to be taken in the morning, afternoon, evening, and at bedtime. This is especially effective for the members with memory loss. This type of pharmacy dispensary may prevent the member from neglecting to take their medication if they need to self-administer it prior to the HHA arriving.

For a member who is unable to recall medication schedules, the HHA should be scheduled to arrive at a member's home prior to their administration of medication. This will confirm the member is taking their medication as ordered. The HHA must be able to confirm the information on the label and the member's comprehension.

Changes in Independence

Reporting of areas such as independent verses dependent skill performance can be done accurately by an HHA who predominantly cares for and observes the member under all circumstances. An example would be if a member was oriented to time, date, and place as some of the indicators. However, there are members who may need to be reminded. This level of evaluation can be finalized with the member's capabilities of recalling current events. This may be the only deficit the member may have, which can also be termed "short-term memory loss."

Frequency of such loss of short-term memory can be harmful to self or others, as in dementia. The member may need assistance in areas such as medication, reminders, and meal preparation. Until the role description for HHA medication administration becomes a standard of practice, it will be preferred that a licensed RN be assigned management to perform that duty, as with a pill box or pharmacy dispensing individually packaged daily medication.

A call-reminding system may also be another way to help those who are highly prone to forgetting their medication schedules. This system can be evaluated for its efficacy for members who do not have support systems in place, live alone, and have difficulty with short-term memory.

To be cost-effective, we will need to revisit the master care plan that is left in a member's home at the start of home care services. The model for home care services for the Medicaid member should be revisited and revised. It is my hope that we will see both Medicare and Medicaid patients receiving the same opportunities to live a fulfilled life in the comfort of their homes.

CHAPTER SEVEN

ULTIMATE RESPONSIBILITY AND RECOMMENDATIONS

HHAs are the eyes and ears for the agency and ultimately the taxpayer. Preserving the integrity of those involved in the home care industry entails all who have a responsibility in home care services to follow the proper standards of practice that regulate the home care service.

The decision to receive HHA services may begin by a medical professional, a family member, or the patient themselves. The decision could be right or wrong. The final monitoring of this would be on the home care agency to decide whether it is appropriate to continue services or not.

Need for Stricter Guidelines

Earlier, we discussed the discrepancies with the field nurse, the educator, and the CEO of a home care agency. A visit to the patients' homes begins with a request for home care services requested by the private MD assigned to that patient. Two decades ago, the request was forwarded to the assigned healthcare provider of that member. The Medicaid private care physician used Medicaid guidelines to approve the need for home care services. Back then, the physician did not feel so obligated to approve home care services, as it is today, to keep the member from leaving their medical services.

However, some MDs who will adhere to the Medicaid regulations, risking the loss of the member to another doctor with a more lenient practice. The patient who was under the Medicaid benefits program was not likely to jump from doctor to doctor in an attempt to find an approval for Medicaid services. In the state of New Jersey, the HMO, as of 2011, would assign either United Healthcare, Horizon New Jersey, Well Care, or Amerigroup to every approved Medicaid recipient under the Medicaid regulations and protocols. The HMO may differ from state to state.

It wasn't long before the members could master how to simply ask their private physician for home care services and receive them. If they were denied a request from the private physician, they would just move on to another healthcare provider. I noted major discrepancies from the time patients were no longer simply Medicare/Medicaid recipients but instead were assigned to a provider under the HMO.

The member can be denied a request for services early in the process by their private physician who would assess that the member can assist themselves with the ADL. Many years ago, it was likely that the member would accept the physician's decision or transfer to another healthcare provider in the hope of obtaining approval. If the denial was due to the health insurance plan final outcome assessment, the member may choose to transfer to another health insurance. The business of gaining another member would get the patient approved.

There is certainly a major disconnect between the health insurance providers. The cause for denial requires a protocol that first needs to be reinforced by the Medicaid home care assistance program. Every healthcare provider needs stricter guidelines before approving the home care based on need versus business and want. Newer and stricter guidelines will decrease the fraudulent use of home care services by the Medicaid population and the health insurance provider.

Currently, the guidelines do not delineate or include how the patient manages with personal care services twenty-four hours a day. For example, if the member has services three hours a day, Monday through Friday, how do they manage with personal care, meal preparation, and light housekeeping when the HHA is not there?

What are the essential ADL that a member cannot safely complete within twenty-four hours a day, seven days per week? Does the patient live by themselves, and are there others who can attend to the member's personal needs?

Asking Better Questions

The RN assessor must be able to ascertain what part of the day will not be assisted by the HHA, which may require a report to Adult Protective Services. The member can be approved for an assignment of three to four hours a day. Assessment questions and supervision at the time of the assessment is crucial.

- What is the mental orientation of the individual?
- Is it mild, moderate, or severe memory loss?
- Is there a diagnosis of dementia or Alzheimer's?
- Does the member have other social or family support?
- Are there medical findings or activities supporting a change in mental status?
- Is there independent use of upper and lower extremities?
- Does the member attend an adult day care program? If so, is the member independent with morning activities in preparation for the adult day care transportation?
- What kind of assistance is required for the member to attend the adult day care?

- Is the member able to assist themselves with personal care prior to being picked up by the adult day care?
- Can the patient manage with ADL by themselves twenty-four hours per day if services were not approved?
- What are the reasons the member is seeking home care services?
- Can the services be met by other support members? Why or why not?
- Which schedule is the member requesting? For example: morning, late morning, afternoon, or late afternoon.
- What are their physical or motor limitations?

The need of the home care service and its policies require a continuity of unbiased review of the approval for the award of service and the need for the home care services. This will require independent review from the accreditation auditing committee and the auditing of the HMO for the indicators used to approve the home care services. Currently, I do not know of an auditing committee or a surveyor reviewing for fraudulent use of the Medicaid-approved home care services. However, the surveyor would site the agency for the lack of personal care documentation and remind the agency's Director of Nursing of the need to document personal care needs to comply with Medicaid regulations.

In summary, the completed HMO approval must align with the home health agency nurse's assessment. The RN's assessment should be the requirement for payment instead of the HHA's daily reporting activity sheet, which may fraudulently document that personal care was rendered.

Home care services are mocked as being housekeeping as opposed to a service in which the goals are to maintain nutrition, normal body function, and mobility of the muscular-skeletal system. The housekeeping and babysitting of a member are against the Medicaid protocol. In clarification, the HHA will assume light housekeeping as their job description when it entails washing the member's dishes after preparing a meal or cleaning a commode or bathtub on a weekly basis to prevent bacteria and infection.

There is an increase in the unstable older population of both Medicaid and non-Medicaid status. Who will be the caregiver when a seventy-year-old cannot attend to their ninety-year-old mother? The guidelines probably won't consider the elderly home alone without anyone to make decisions or help them with their daily needs.

I continue to inquire of both the home health agencies and the state government officials about their potential plans to protect the elderly from premature deterioration due to lack of medical intervention and the needed home care services.

Updating the Tool

We can begin to have an assessment tool that would immediately identify those members who have not seen any social support for several weeks. The assessment tool suggested should be made available to all social and medical professionals such as doctors, nurses, home healthcare agencies, medical clinics, and social workers. It would be the private care physician, nurse practitioner, or physician's assistant who would complete the tool for the request of services. These professionals can identify which group of individuals are missed, regardless of their income or medical insurance status.

Here are some general aspects that should be investigated by the assessment tool:

- living accommodations: alone or with others
- ambulatory ability
- ability to move safely in and out of wheelchair or bed
- supportive services in place
- the availability of personal supportive services
- ability to assist self with light meal preparation
- ability to assist self with medication
- the mental comprehension or orientation to recall current and past events
- the ability to maintain an optimum level of health with minimal assistance of support systems such as a family member or home care individual

The assessment tool may help indicate the events that will require assistance for a member on a day-to-day basis. We should keep in mind some members are independent with personal care; however, they may need help with shopping and light housekeeping. Then it would be cost-effective for those approving the award of service to approve a group of hours once weekly and not daily for services or as a point of care assistance.

The following can be customized for the individual because not all will require every service listed:

- meal preparation—one to three meals per day
- bathing
- medication assistance
- shopping
- medical follow-up appointments where a telehealth review cannot be applied

The RN is required to do a visit every sixty days or as needed, prior to the fifty-day mark. The RN employed by the home health agency that requires a sixty-day visit is to identify the necessity of the home health services or the improvement and independence of ADL. The nurse should be able to assess the member for the past, present, and up to the next sixty days. The member may require home care assistance to reach an optimum level of health or until there is overall independence on the ADL. It is the RN's assessment that will identify any improvement in the general health goals.

- Self-care deficiencies are reduced.
- There is maximum independence.
- The member is able to maintain nutritional intake.
- The member can maintain a safe environment.

The goals mentioned should be divided into a twenty-four-hour period. If the member lives alone, the self-care needed should be calculated into a certain number of hours to indicate what ADL the member is capable of safely attending to. If the member requires assistance with ADL, the RN using the follow-up assessment tool can identify any improvements or deficiencies in their level of independence with their personal care.

The assessment tool should clearly indicate which skills require supervision or assistance when the HHA is present. The tool will also report to the HMO those members who require a reduction or increase in the award of service hours. The integrity of the RN's professional assessment will determine the outcome of the continued care. If completed accurately, the assessment tool will score the member's results showing required continued care or the approval of services. In my experience, the assessment tool may have better outcomes if done by an organization independent of the HMO and home care agency.

The protocol realistically examines how frequently ADL are required. The approval for service has alterations as to how an individual, dependent or independent, performs before or after the HHA schedule. If a member has service from 6:00 p.m. to 8:00 p.m., this only requires assistance with one meal per day. This is exactly the reason why the evaluation currently done is not compliant for meeting the care of the patient. In this case, we are speaking of the elderly people who live by themselves.

Reassess Meal System

Meals on Wheels is a remedy to the member who needs assistance with meals, but it is of great concern because these aren't the healthiest of meals. For example, I have seen the prepared boxes for diabetic patients include things like pancakes, mashed potatoes, and other foods known to elevate blood sugar levels. Meals can be delivered, but there cannot be any compromise in its preparation. The activity of bathing is a hands-on activity where human hands are needed. Bathing does not have to be at 6:00 a.m. or 6:00 p.m. The member must acknowledge the service is a Medicaid-paid service when the regulations are applied. The goal is to prevent falls and unnecessary hospitalizations.

There is too much liberty with patients' requests. The member needs to be lenient with what is available at the time of the contract. This type of ad-lib request by the member makes the point of care suggested in this chapter difficult to implement. The home health agency should be able to identify the HHA available and attempt to provide the member with the appropriate service. The Medicaid recipient does not pay for the services. The member must allow accommodations of the home healthcare agency or be denied the services.

CONCLUSION

The fast growth of the less-active elderly population calls for the immediate attention for enhancing independence with self-care. It challenges the importance of how to maintain the optimum health for today's growing elderly population. Many of the elderly are living to the age of eighty-five or older. Their sons and daughters are considered senior citizens, exhibiting comorbidity themselves, and are unable to care for their elderly parents as primary caregivers.

The paid caregivers are only available to the very rich when privately paid or to the very poor when approved by the Medicaid managed health organization assigned to the different providers under health managed insurance. Some commonly known companies are United Health Care, Well Care, Horizon, and Amerigroup, which may differ from state to state.

The Medicaid HMO home healthcare services are only offered to those living at the poverty level. This excludes some recipients who may live minimally above the poverty level. They are typically denied Medicaid services for home health or may have only Medicare benefits that will not approve long-term care for home care services.

The tools currently used for the assessment by the individual HMO are not capable of identifying fraudulent activity by the RN assessor, recipient, and assigned home healthcare agency. Suggestions for assessments provided in this book were findings I noted as the owner of a home health agency, a home health instructor, and the hired field supervisor for various home health agencies. This experience allowed me the diversity to covertly gather the findings illustrated in this book. The overt or obviously accepted fraudulent activity has become the accepted standard of practice of home care approval or denial of an award that assigns the hours of service.

HHAs are the eyes and the ears for the patient, the home health agency, and the state. The HHA does not have the support or the reward required for the reporting of fraudulent events in the field of home care. The fear of losing credibility and their employment outweighs the challenges and outcomes of reporting and proving the facts, which would require a nonbiased assessment and another model indicating actual points of care and need. The organization is to begin with the Board of Nursing at the level of recognizing that HHAs are the frontline essential workers of the home care industry with an established Code of Ethics for adherence and accountability of the following:

- report any acts of fraudulent activity contrary to the policy and procedures and the scope of practice
- adhere to the plan of care as instructed by the RN
- keep the patient's information confidential
- protect the patient of nonmaleficence (to do no harm)
- practice within the job description for the HHA and within the scope of practice
- adhere to the laws and ethics applicable to the role of the HHA
- acknowledge the client's Bill of Rights
- report negligence and abuse immediately

The HHA plays a major role in the daily care and protection of the elderly and disabled individuals. They have chosen this profession but have felt very much abandoned by the home care industry system. Every day, they risk their lives, health, and dignity behind the closed doors of patients' homes. This risk was even more profound during the COVID-19 pandemic. They want to be recognized as the healthcare workers who work for the elderly and the disabled with humility, not humiliation.

ABOUT THE AUTHOR

Evelyn Vargas became interested in elder care through church ministry at the age of thirteen. She followed that interest and became a licensed practical nurse at the age of eighteen. She advanced her career as a registered nurse specializing in emergency room nursing while also pursuing a career in home care nursing.

In 2005, she opened Serenity Home Health Services, a privately-owned agency, and loved not only helping its members but also those in her employ. Over time, she became aware of the fraud and dishonesty in the government-paid programs and closed the agency, which led her to write about her experiences. It is her passionate desire to raise awareness of this malfeasance while protecting the dignity of home health aides and their contribution of caring for the elder community.

ENDNOTES

1 Flavia Medrut. "13 Inspirational Florence Nightingale Quotes to Nurse Your Soul." *Goalcast*, 20 Apr. 2021, https://www.goalcast.com/2018/02/08/inspirational-florence-nightingale-quotes/. *Contents.* https://www.un.org/en/events/pastevents/pdfs/Madrid_plan.pdf.

2 *Contents.* https://www.un.org/en/events/pastevents/pdfs/Madrid_plan.pdf.

3 Cobb, Daniel. "Medicaid & Home Care: State by State Benefits & Eligibility." *Payment Options & Financial Assistance for Senior Care*, PayingforSeniorCare.com, 25 June 2021, https://www.payingforseniorcare.com/medicaid-waivers/home-care. This link will explain the Medicaid benefits.

4 "The Nightingale Pledge." *The Truth About Nursing*, https://www.truthaboutnursing.org/press/pioneers/nightingale_pledge.html. Accessed 28 Sept. 2021.

Made in the USA
Monee, IL
04 November 2026

67379278R00075